THE
MASTER

To Star,
Don't search far for
what lies near.
Don't seek what already
is here

Blessings & Bliss

THE
MASTER

Parables for
Enlightenment

KEVIN EDWARDS

Printed in the United States of America.

Cover design by David Ruppe, Impact Publications
Cover: *Autumn Trinity* by Mara Friedman
Author photo by Dierdre Hauflaire
Interior design by Christy Collins

Library of Congress Cataloging-in-Publication Data

Edwards, Kevin.
The Master : parables for enlightenment / by Kevin Edwards.
p. cm. Includes bibliographical references.
ISBN 1-883991-65-X (pbk.)
1. Spiritual life. 2. Parables. I. Title.
BL624.2.E39 2004
204'.4--dc22   2004012825

Acknowledgements

❀ I WOULD LIKE TO THANK MY PARENTS, Mike and Lenore, for their love and support, along with Michael Leach, Brother Wayne Teasdale, Rev. Richard De Ranitz, Fr. Paul Burak, Fr. John Karondukadavil, Fr. Isaiah Ovonji, Rev. Paul Murray, Fr. Peter Rookey, Mother Elisabetta Patrizi, Marcia Hauflaire, Marilyn Eubanks, Philamine Scervino, Matthew Kelly, Tom Skorupa, and Megan Mele.

Subversive Wisdom

✤ PARABLES HAVE LONG BEEN CENTRAL to spiritual teaching. Jesus, Buddha, the great rabbis of the Kabbalah, Zen masters and Sufi shaykhs and pirs have all been drawn to the form of the parable as a teaching tool. At the heart of the parable (from the Greek *parabole*) is comparison. Traditionally, a parable gives us a short teaching that draws on everyday experience to reach out to a deeper, spiritual lesson, be it ethical or mystical. A master teacher speaks of common events that everyone understands as part of society's stock of conventional wisdom. And then the master finds a way to undermine the expected truth with a healthy dose of subversive wisdom.

Kevin Edwards' takes this ancient form of spiritual teaching and focuses the parable to a particular aim: to turn the reader toward the mystical. Edwards does this in a manner that is both exciting and perfectly suited to our moment in time.

In this small but deep volume, the Master is not a speaker from the distant past, but is very much a contemporary figure, telling stories from our time and about our time, addressing our present-day concerns. The Master, however, is not a historical figure, but a shape-shifting figure who sometimes speaks as a woman and sometimes as a man. But with each parable, the Master brings us into a new relationship with the One. In other words, the true Master is a teacher who is not terribly concerned about a systematic or an orthodox theology, but rather is all about helping us see existence in the light of oneness, and to taste (as the Sufis would say) the sweetness of our true, our divine nature.

Edwards' parables are compelling because his subversive Sage invites those who hear them to live their lives in a spiritual universe that is at home in the world yet at odds against conventional wisdom and even more so conventional religion. The Master and the awakened student are radicals who more often than not undermine the conventional through humility and reverence toward all creation.

Steven Scholl

The Garden

IT BEGAN IN A GARDEN. He had knowledge of his surroundings but knew not who he was. "Perhaps I am a rock," thought the boy, so he stood very still alongside the rock and tried not to move. But the wind came and blew the boy down, so he gave up the idea that he might be a rock. He traveled a little further and stopped before a tree. "Perhaps I am a tree," he thought to himself. Swaying back and forth, the boy stood alongside the tree, but although he stretched out his arms, he did not sprout leaves, and so gave up the idea that he might be the tree. He pondered the question again as he made his way to the river. "Perhaps I am the river. For the river has a mouth as do I." But the following week there came a drought and the river dried up, so the boy gave up the idea that he might be the river and continued his search. For many years, he did not know how to answer the question, "Who am I?" Still, he continued to journey through the Garden and inquire. "Perhaps I am the canyon. For the canyon is hollow and empty inside, and that is how I feel." He looked up at the sun. Never had he seen anything more beautiful. "Perhaps I am the sun." He cherished the thought, but eventually the sun went down into the night sky, and the boy gave up the idea that he might be the sun. "The wind!" he thought. "Perhaps I am the wind." But the wind is unbounded and free, and so he gave up the idea that he might be the wind. When he had exhausted all possible choices, his heart quietly spoke to him. "You are the rock, for the true Self is sturdy, stable, and firm. And you are the tree, for it is the nature of the true Self to bear much fruit. And you are the river, for your true Self is one with the source. And you are the canyon, for your true Self is bottomless and unfathomable. And you are the sun, for your true Self is the light of the world. And you are the wind, for the true Self is unbounded and free."

**There is nothing negative about
having a negative knowledge of one's self.**

☾ ☾ ☾ ☾

*To know what you are,
you must first investigate and know what you are not.*
SRI NISARGADATTA MAHARAG

The Right Disposition

✸ WHEN ASKED WHETHER GOD favored churchgoers over non-churchgoers, the Master told this story. "A young man set out in search of lasting bliss. He went first to the brothels, second to the pubs, third to the casinos, and lastly to the neighborhood church. When the service ended, immediately he approached the minister. 'Everything I was searching for, I found within these walls,' exclaimed the young man. 'Tell me more,' said the minister. 'Well, it was just like the brothels in that there were many beautiful women, and it was just like the pubs in that they served good tasting wine, and it was just like the casinos in that when I recited the creed no one could tell I was bluffing.'"

**Without the right disposition,
going to church no more makes you a saint
than swimming in water makes you a fish.**

☾ ☾ ☾ ☾

*An hour is coming, and now is, when the true worshipers
will worship the Father in spirit and truth;
for such people the Father seeks to be His worshipers.*
JOHN 4:23

Two Flute Players

❋ TWO FLUTE PLAYERS PERFORMED day and night in the market-place. From sunup to sundown they each drew their share of listeners. Though both were successful, they differed greatly in their approach. While the one played sublimely, he had the habit of playing softly, and only those who drew near could relish the beautiful song. The other, a far less talent, garnered his share by playing loudly and always the same tune. Those who had an ear for music renounced the crude and repetitious sounds for the more harmonious ones, but the others became accustomed to the harsher tones because they were louder and more familiar.

**When you are in concert with God, discernment
is simple. Recognizing the tune of Love,
you refuse all contrary sounds.**

☾ ☾ ☾ ☾

The flute of the infinite is played without ceasing and its sound is love.
KABIR

Not the Storm

❀ THE MASTER GATHERED her disciples on a mountaintop and began to teach them. "The true Self," she said, "lies beyond both thoughts and feelings. That is why it is unaffected by sadness, anxiety, confusion, or fear." When asked how one arrives at this state, she responded, "Like a rainbow, it appears after the storm. You must pass through the storm to get there. But only the one who knows that he is not the storm may pass through it."

**The seer meets the slightest ripples
and the greatest storms with equal ease.**

❨ ❨ ❨ ❨

*Behold, there arose a great storm on the sea,
so that the boat was being covered with the waves;
but Jesus Himself was asleep.*
MATTHEW 8: 24–26

Trusting Oneself

❋ THAT THE KING HAD MANY counselors was not a positive thing, since when it came time for him to decide, he knew not which course of action to take. While one counseled to raise taxes, the other counseled to lower taxes. While one counseled to make peace, another counseled to wage war. This caused the king distress and confusion, so he sought the opinion of the hired help. He went first to the gardener, next to the housekeeper, and last to the cook. After recounting his dilemma, the cook looked up at the king, paused, and began to speak. "I am just a simple cook and know nothing of politics or ruling a kingdom, but I know well how to cook and prepare soup, and I know that a hearty soup requires many different ingredients and spices. But were I not to season the broth myself, it would be either too spicy or too salty or too bland." The king took the advice of the cook, and from then on, although he conferred with others, he trusted himself.

The Counselor, who is not you, is present within you.

☾ ☾ ☾ ☾

Wisdom will enter your heart, and knowledge will be pleasant to your soul.
Discretion will protect you, and understanding will guard you.
PROVERBS 2:10–11

Stoked

⊛ A MAN WENT TO SEE THE MASTER to work through his issues with anger. He talked and vented for over an hour as the Master quietly listened. When the hour was up, the Master asked, "How do you feel?" "Lighter," the man replied. "You were exasperated and now you are lighter. Do you know why?" The man paused. Then the Master spoke, "A fire left to burn will die of its own accord, so it is with anger if not stoked by unnecessary words."

Either your words provoke, or they pacify.

❰ ❰ ❰ ❰

A gentle answer turns away wrath, but a harsh word stirs up anger.
PROVERBS 15:1–2

Whose Feelings?

❋ A HEATED ARGUMENT broke out and a couple flew into a rage. They sought help from the village counselor, who taught them how to communicate. The key was not to blame one another, but only to express feelings. They thanked him and both left convinced they had received something of value. A week passed and the couple found themselves in another argument. They tried the formula but it didn't seem to have the same effect. Gradually, conflict increased and the relationship grew worse. They went to see the village counselor, but he had taken ill. Confused as to what they might do, they sought out an insightful woman who lived at the edge of town. The woman listened as the couple took turns speaking. Finally, she interrupted. "Forgive me if I seem insensitive, but whose feelings are hurting you?" "I don't understand," the couple responded. She repeated the question. "Whose feelings are hurting you? Are they your spouse's feelings, or are they yours?" "I suppose they're mine," each one answered. "Then take responsibility for what is yours, and let your spouse do the same. No one is responsible for how you feel." Suddenly, how the couple might solve their problem was no longer a concern. There was no longer a problem to solve.

**If hurt is so disagreeable to you,
why do you so readily agree to feel it?**

❨ ❨ ❨ ❨

No one can make you feel inferior without your consent.
ELEANOR ROOSEVELT

Who am I?

✵ TWO BROTHERS GREW to be actors. They starred in everything from comedies to tragedies, always competing for the leading role. As success and stardom began to take hold, one of the boys was approached by a prestigious talent agency. They changed his name, made over his image, and promoted him as a sex symbol. The other was faced with the same options but did not succumb. When asked how he withstood the social pressures and demands, he simply responded, "Though I was cast in numerous roles, there was one question I never stopped asking: 'Who am I?'"

**In times of confusion,
it is enough to ask one question.**

❰ ❰ ❰ ❰

Give up all questions except one: 'Who am I?'
After all, the only fact you are sure of is that you are.
The 'I am' is certain. The 'I am this' is not.
Struggle to find out what you are in reality.
SRI NISARGADATTA MAHARAG

The Master's Ale

✺ A NUMBER OF VILLAGERS went to see the Master who was believed to have a cure for nightmares. "Sorry to trouble you," they said. "But we have not had a good night's rest for quite some time." The Master stood silent as she listened to each of their stories, then led with a simple question. "During the hours you are awake, what are you not properly addressing?" "What do you mean?" they asked. "No matter," she replied. She then proceeded to mix the medicine. "Drink this ale twice a day." Each of them left with the prescribed ale, but the Master's question refused to leave: During the hours you are awake, what are you not properly addressing? Day by day they drank the ale and day by day the nightmares decreased, and all throughout, the Master's question did not leave. A month went by and the villagers returned to acquire more ale. "Your ale is truly powerful, could you mix us some more?" "I will mix another quart of ale if you like," replied the Master, "but the power is not in the ale, it's in the question."

No darkness can withstand the light of awareness.

❨ ❨ ❨ ❨

Awareness is the path of immortality;
thoughtlessness is the path of death.
SIDDHARTHA GAUTAMA

The Ballet

✸ WHEN THE BALLET WASN'T QUITE coming together, the producer went to consult a well-known dance choreographer, who agreed to help ready the dancers. After just a short while, the show opened as scheduled and received rave reviews. Accordingly, they celebrated their success and toasted the dance choreographer whose cunning prepared the dancers in just days. When asked how he was able to pull it off. He sheepishly replied, "I sped up the tempo."

**Life is like a ballet, quicken the pace and
it becomes difficult to uncover hidden faults.**

❨ ❨ ❨ ❨

*We first have to be able to sit back and examine ourselves
with detachment and search out our patterns of behavior.
Paradoxically, people who hurry are actually stuck in the same spot.*
EKNATH EASWARAN

The Journey

✳ A GROUP OF MEN set off on an arduous journey to a distant land. But from the very moment their journey began, their number began to dwindle. "We cannot cross rivers and streams," said a few, so they quit and turned back. Others remarked, "Surely we cannot cross these mountains," and they, too, turned back. Still others said, "What will become of us if we are lost in the forest?" And they turned back as well. Still others remarked, "Should we perish in the desert, what then?" And they returned with the rest. But a remnant persevered. They successfully crossed rivers and streams, mountains and deserts, forests and open plains, until finally they reached the distant land. Word was sent back that they had completed their journey. Friends, family members, and reporters prepared for their return. Upon their arrival, a young man pushed through the dense crowd and fired a question, "How did you succeed? How were you able to meet such challenges, when so many could not?" The travelers responded, "As far as we can tell, we had only one advantage. Where others saw obstacles, we saw opportunities."

Listening to God means ignoring all the voices that say, "It's impossible."

☾ ☾ ☾ ☾

Our duty, as men and women, is to proceed
as if limits to our ability did not exist...
PIERRE TEILHARD DE CHARDIN

Dropping Desire

A YOUNG DISCIPLE APPROACHED the Master and asked, "Why is it that 'desire' is seen by the great teachers as negative?" The Master corrected the boy, saying, "Not all desires are seen in this way, only some." When the boy asked which ones, the Master replied, "Only the ones which cause suffering." He then told this story. "There was a man in the village whose only desire was to be rich. Born of lower middle class, he came to believe from an early age all that mattered in life was success and money. But no matter what he tried, success did not find him. Finally, after considerable failure, he came to see that the only obstacle that stood between himself and happiness was desire, so he dropped his desire and found happiness."

As a general rule, all desires are positive until you come up against something you can't have or don't need.

☾ ☾ ☾ ☾

Hope deferred makes the heart sick,
but desire fulfilled is a tree of life.
PROVERBS 13:12

Religion and Spirituality

✺ A DISCUSSION AROSE regarding religion and spirituality. Whereas some saw the two as separate and totally unrelated, others saw them as united and complementary. To settle the dispute, the Master told this story. "Two sisters grew to be very fond of music. Wherever they went they were found either singing or whistling their favorite song. Over time, the older sister developed slightly greater talent. So the younger said to herself, "What is to keep me from surpassing my older sister?" And she hollowed out a reed and fashioned a flute. "This instrument will give shape and form to my breath and will make up for all that I lack." "So it is with religion," the Master added. "It gives shape and form to the breath of the Spirit."

☾ ☾ ☾ ☾

Religion is the manifestation of the divinity already in man.
SWAMI VIVIKENANDA

The Diver

✻ DEATHLY AFRAID OF THE DEEP, the girl sought to keep her head always above water. She would float on her back, kick her legs, maneuver her arms, anything she could to prevent her going under. Then one day she met a diver, who educated her about certain principles. The diver explained that the force of gravity, which pulled her body down, was equal to that of the water pressure, which pushed it up, and that this was known as the law of neutral buoyancy. The girl left relieved, and from then on let herself sink beneath the water and found it just as the diver had said.

The moralist urges active resistance.
The mystic, passive stillness.

☾ ☾ ☾ ☾

Fear not! Stand your ground and you will see the victory the Lord will win for you today…the Lord himself will fight for you; you have only to keep still.
EXODUS 14:13–15

Truly Paradise

❀ GIVEN A MAP, A MAN went in search of a certain island. Shortly after, it happened that a storm struck, and he found himself shipwrecked, forced to swim ashore. Now without a map or compass, the man resigned to make the best of it. He pitched his tent and began to reflect on the significance of the strange turn of events. Suddenly, he came to realize that the island he happened upon was truly paradise.

**So it is with the journey. Sometimes we are
better off without fair weather, a map,
a compass, or even a destination.**

☾ ☾ ☾ ☾

*One's destination is never a place
but rather a new way of looking at things.*
HENRY MILLER

The Spring

⊛ A YOUNG MAN WENT to see the Master and confided that his feelings were badly hurt. The Master listened, as the boy shared the details of what had happened. When he had finished, the Master posed this question. "Did you ever think it possible that you could be unaffected by both praise and blame?" "Never," he replied. "Well you can, you have only to discover the spring." "What spring?" the boy asked. The Master then told this story. "A certain gardener planted over a spring, a sapling, which grew strong and green. In fact, it grew so strong and so green that the other trees became jealous and envious. One day, their ill will grew so great that they plotted to ruin the young sapling. 'What if it were to rain heavily upon the tree so as to make it drown?' they thought. From then on they beseeched the clouds to make it rain, but the tree only grew greener and sounder. Then they thought to themselves, 'What if it were to grow so dry for the tree so as to make it scorch?' So they beseeched the clouds to withhold their rain, but still the tree thrived. 'How is it,' they asked, 'that the tree still thrives?' And all of them were baffled until they learned of the spring upon which the sapling was planted."

**Beneath the surface of every human being
there is an eternal spring.**

❨ ❨ ❨ ❨

*He will be like a tree planted by the water that sends out its
roots by the stream. It does not fear when heat comes;
its leaves are always green. It has no worries in a
year of drought and never fails to bear fruit.*
JEREMIAH 17:8–9

Conversion

❀ THE MASTER GATHERED a large crowd as she preached to them about conversion. "Conversion," she said, "is only pretend without renunciation." She then told the story of a man who moved from an oceanside residence to a cabin in the mountains. After only a few months, he longed for his former life and returned to the surroundings he had always known. "So it is with conversion," she uttered. "Walking toward can never be done without walking away."

❮ ❮ ❮ ❮

The Lord had said to Abraham, "Leave your country, your people, and your father's household, and go to the land I will show you."
GENESIS 12:1–2

Running Free

✺ A FARMER YOKED A TEAM of horses to a plow in the interest of lightening his workload. Now it turned out that the method worked so well that every farmer did likewise, and for a long time the only horses in the village were fastened to either plows or tills. Then one day, one of the horses broke loose and with lightning speed raced over the hillside. All watched in amazement. "What beauty," they exclaimed, as they beheld for the first time a horse running free.

A truly free person cannot be controlled, nor can he be bought. He submits and is sole owner of himself.

❰ ❰ ❰ ❰

"It shall come about on that day," declares the Lord of hosts, "that I will break his yoke from off their necks and will tear off their bonds; and strangers will no longer make them their slaves."
JEREMIAH 30:8–9

All Brothers

✸ THE MASTER OFTEN SPOKE of rank as a negative thing. When asked why, he told this story: A young boy grew to manhood, but try as he might, he could not grow beyond the anxiety he experienced in the presence of certain individuals. Whenever he confronted anyone who out-ranked him, he immediately felt inferior. Bosses, parents, teachers, anyone who held a position of authority, posed a threat. Then one day, he went to see a monk known for his understanding and insight. The young man explained his situation while the monk listened. When a few minutes had passed, he got up, paged through the scriptures, and gave it to the young man to read.

Do not be called 'Rabbi.' You have but one teacher, and you are all brothers. Call no one on earth your father; you have but one Father in heaven. Do not be called 'Master;' you have but one Master, the Messiah.

When he had finished reading, the man looked up. "There you have it," said the monk. "No mere human being out-ranks you."

❨ ❨ ❨ ❨

I have never, even in my dreams, thought that I was mahatma and that others were alpatma [little soul].
GANDHI

23

Puzzled

⚙ A MAN IN THE VILLAGE was known to have quite a reputation. When the weekend rolled around, he was given either to boozing, gambling, or fornication. Yet after each binge, he was found in the chapel sobbing. Now it happened that one night he got drunk and slept with the minister's daughter. As he lay in her arms, she inquired as to whether he wasn't the man often discovered in the chapel. He admitted he was. She then asked another question. "That you are a man with a reputation is a known fact. That you are a religious man is also known by many, but one thing still puzzles me. What kind of man binds himself to a moral code that he cannot live up to?" He answered, "A principled idealist."

**Nothing is so deadly as duplicity
and nothing so poisonous as ideals.**

❨ ❨ ❨ ❨

*It is the ideal which poisons you and makes you complex,
divides you, makes two persons in you—
the one that you are and the one you would like to be.*
OSHO

A Crisis of Uncertainty

❋ SOUGHT OUT BY MANY for counsel and advice, the Master left her Sundays free for whoever would pay a visit. One morning while tidying up, a young man came to her door. "I no longer know what to do, where to go, what to think, or what to believe," he said. The Master paused, then responded with these words, "To believe one's whole life without a shred of doubt is like trying to play a symphony without rests between notes. It simply cannot be done." From that moment on, the crisis of uncertainty vanished, and the young man left room for self-doubt.

❰ ❰ ❰ ❰

I want to beg you, as much as I can, to be patient toward all that is
unsolved in your heart and try to love the questions themselves like
locked rooms and like books written in a very foreign tongue.
RANIER MARIA RILKE

The Bell Tower

✸ THE MASTER DECIDED TO CLIMB the bell tower and invited a disciple to join him. "No thank you," replied the disciple, "I've already seen the view from the top of the tower." "Indeed, you've seen the view from the top of the tower," said the Master, "but you've not seen the view from the top of the tower this day." "True," said the disciple, "but I have seen it on similar days." At that, the Master grew angry and struck the disciple freely. "You've not learned one thing since you came here," said the Master. "Life is now. Stop living on memories!" Shortly after, the Master died, and his disciples had his final words inscribed on his headstone. In bold letters they wrote the following: "I've seen that before, I've tasted that before, I've heard that before, I've felt that before, we've met before. These are the words of one who will never re-enter childhood."

Familiarity is a barrier to experiencing
each moment with freshness.

❰ ❰ ❰ ❰

To live completely, wholly, every day as if it were a new loveliness,
there must be dying to everything of yesterday, otherwise you live
mechanically, and a mechanical mind can never know
what love is or what freedom is.
J. KRISHNAMURTI

Tiny Gold Granules

✸ THE DISCIPLES OFTEN COMPLAINED about distractions during meditation. "No such thing," the Master replied. When they asked what she meant, she told a story about a woman who went down to the river to pan for gold. She took her sieve and straightway immersed it in the water. After just a few seconds, she pulled it out and sifted through sediment until she beheld tiny gold granules. "So it is with meditation," said the Master. "What you refer to as distraction is a key component, just as sifting through sediment is essential in panning for gold."

**Movements of the mind become distractions
when you resist instead of watch them,
when you oppose instead of observe.**

❨ ❨ ❨ ❨

*In true meditation all objects are left to their natural functioning.
This means that no effort should be made to manipulate or
suppress any object of awareness. In true meditation the emphasis
is on being awareness: Not on being aware of objects,
but on resting as primordial awareness itself.*
ADYASHANTI

Transformation

❀ THE MASTER OFTEN TAUGHT that transformation was effortless, which was why it was so difficult to achieve. When pressed for an explanation, she immediately left the room and returned with a spotlight and a prism. She turned off the lights, shined the spotlight at the prism, pointed, and said, "That is transformation, yet the prism does nothing except receive light." And they questioned her no further.

**The transformation that is required
is the transformation of consciousness,
which comes about through non–effort.**

☾ ☾ ☾ ☾

Be still and know that I am God.
PSALM 46:11

True Self-Control

✸ WHENEVER PROVOKED, THE YOUNG LAD cursed his fellow man. Should the occasion arise, derogatory remarks would spew from his mouth like venom. It grew to such an extent that perfect strangers began to reprove the young man. "Change your tone," said one. "Watch your mouth," said another. "Control your tongue," said a third. Then came a fourth and final voice. "Better yet, more than your mouth, watch your inner dialogue, more than your tone, change your thoughts. More than your tongue, control your cruelty."

**True self-control is not suppressed
behavior but enlightenment.**

❰ ❰ ❰ ❰

*The wise who control their body, who control their tongue,
the wise who control their mind are truly well controlled.*
SIDDHARTHA GAUTAMA

The Artifact

❋ "WHILE DOING AN EXCAVATION, a group of villagers stumbled upon what appeared to be a mysterious artifact. Immediately they took it to the lab to run a series of tests. When the relic proved to be from antiquity, experts were called in to decipher its meaning. First, mathematicians were called in to crack possible secret codes. Then, archeologists were summoned to expound on the significance of the strange markings. Soon, articles emerged commenting on the placement of each marking and symbol, and eventually, whole books were written elucidating an alleged secret message. Cults and study groups sprung up centered around the strange scrawl. Years passed, and immigrants came over from far away lands. As a result, the villagers were introduced to a variety of lifestyles, languages, and cultures. Eventually, they learned that the ancient relic was just a simple road sign. The Master often told this story to his disciples who, as he put it, "Delighted in the esoteric and dismissed the ordinary."

❮ ❮ ❮ ❮

The invariable mark of wisdom is to
see the miraculous in the common.
RALPH WALDO EMERSON

The Glass Cleaner

✵ THE MASTER OFTEN SAID that time could be better spent looking inward than outward. When asked what he meant, he said, "A glass cleaner erected scaffolding and proceeded to climb toward the few windows that were out of reach. When he arrived, he took his sponge, soaked the glass, and ran his squeegee. But the glass didn't wash clean. After just a few attempts, he realized that the dirt was on the inside." "So it is with each of us," the Master added. "Which is why we must turn our attention inward."

❨ ❨ ❨ ❨

Why do you look at the speck that is in your brother's eye,
but do not notice the log that is in your own eye?
MATTHEW 7:3

The Chant

✸ THE MASTER WAS KNOWN to have a chant that, when recited, had the effect of instantly changing the world for the better. When villagers caught wind of this, they immediately flocked to his doorstep. "What do you seek?" he asked. "We seek to learn the chant that changes the world for the better," they responded. "I know of such a chant," he replied. "So powerful it is to change the world for the better, but so reluctant are people to use it." "Not us," said the villagers. "We promise to put it to good use." At that, the Master agreed to teach them. "Very well, repeat these words: How – can – I – help – you? Now use them as often as you feel the need to change the world for the better."

❬ ❬ ❬ ❬

Man's triumph will consist in substituting the struggle
for existence with a struggle for mutual service.
GANDHI

One Great Sin

✺ HAVING LEARNED OF A CERTAIN monk's ability to read hearts, the young woman traveled almost a full day's journey. When she finally arrived, she begged to know the extent of her sinfulness. The monk turned to her with seriousness and said, "I see one great sin." "What is it?" she asked. "That, in possession of a beautiful garden, your only concern is for compost, that in possession of a priceless heirloom, your only concern is dust."

**Time is not well spent looking at sins,
but looking past them.**

❨ ❨ ❨ ❨

*He does not treat us as our sins deserve or
repay us according to our iniquities.*
PSALM 103:10

Taking Inventory

⊛ A CERTAIN OWNER of a cannery decided that to better compete with other companies, he would, once a month, do a complete inventory of his stock. When the end of the first month rolled around, he found the task futile, since a large percentage of the cans were unmarked.

**Without the proper labels, taking a
mental inventory is equally impossible.**

❨ ❨ ❨ ❨

*We need to clearly identify different mental states and
make a distinction, classifying them according to
whether they lead to happiness or not.*
TENZIN GYATSO

Footnotes

✸ WHEN HIS DISCIPLES asked why so few appreciated the beauty of nature, the Master responded, "For the same reason few appreciate the beauty of Scripture, because they fail to read the footnotes." "Footnotes?" they asked. The Master then pointed to the twilight sky. "In this case they read, ALL FOR YOU MY CHILD, ALL FOR YOU!" Until that moment, the disciples had not truly seen a sunset.

You are seeing things as they are, when you sense outrageous Love all around you.

❨ ❨ ❨ ❨

The earth is full of His unfailing love.
PSALM 33:5

The Missionary

❋ AN EAGER YOUNG MISSIONARY was sent overseas to preach the good news. But wherever he went, he met with resistance. "You will be hated by all because of my name," he thought to himself, and so he made little of it. But as time passed, the villagers grew to vehemently despise the young missionary, which only strengthened his resolve. Eventually, the missionary died and was brought to judgment, where there appeared before him a large scroll. Upon it was written, "You will be hated by all because of me." Believing this to be his rite of passage, at once he sought to enter paradise, when suddenly there came a voice. "Not you. You were hated for other reasons."

When the crusaders came, they brought bloodshed.
When the angels came, they brought tidings of great joy.

❨ ❨ ❨ ❨

How beautiful are the feet of those who bring good news!
ROMANS 10:15

The Critic

✸ A FAMOUS FOOD CRITIC sat down to dinner. Moments later, the chef came over and recommended the seared Ahi Tuna, which was the house special. The critic agreed, and when the food was ready, the server brought it to the table with a complimentary glass of wine. So savory was the entrée that the critic moaned after each bite. Finally, another diner spoke out. "I see you ordered the special. How is it?" she asked. "Wonderfully delicious," he replied. "Would you like a taste?" "No, I will take your word for it. After all, you're the critic."

**The goodness of the Lord is not something
you take one's word for, but something
you must taste for yourself.**

❨ ❨ ❨ ❨

No one can chew your food for you.
PRAKASH

The Invitation

✸ A SIZABLE GROUP, GOING into town, invited the Master to join them. Without the slightest hesitation, he declined and went his way. All were taken aback by the abrupt response, and throughout the evening, their attention centered on the Master's quick departure. "I expected more from such a holy man," said one, and before long he was judged to be terse, rude, and insensitive. But as the criticisms mounted, they noticed one among them uncharacteristically silent. "What is your opinion of the Master?" they asked. "Would you like my opinion or my observation?" replied the man. "What do you mean? You saw the same as we," they retorted. "On the contrary, you saw a man who was selfish, I saw one who was self-directed."

**You cannot betray others by being true to your Self,
nor can you be true to others by betraying your Self.**

❨ ❨ ❨ ❨

*This above all, to thine own self be true, and it must follow,
as the night the day, thou canst not then be false to any man.*
WILLIAM SHAKESPEARE

The Costume

❀ A MAN WAS INVITED to a costume party, and so went in search of a costume. He came upon the first storefront he spotted and asked, "Excuse me, but where can I purchase a costume?" "Just a mile down the road," the storeowner replied. "You'll see the sign." The man politely thanked the storeowner aand advanced down the road. When he had gone about a mile he discovered an enormous sign, "Costumes and Suits for Sale!" Relieved, the man entered the store but saw nothing but three-piece suits. Puzzled, he approached the storeowner. "Pardon me sir, but where the devil are your costumes?" "That depends on you," the storeowner replied. "What do you mean it depends on me? What depends on me?" asked the man. The storeowner looked the man up and down. "42 regular?" he asked. "Correct," said the man. The storeowner then handed him his size. "If, when you put it on, you become self-possessed, then it is a suit; if you become self-conscious, it is a costume."

Both the body and clothing are costumes.

❮ ❮ ❮ ❮

Save the image, lose the man. Lose the image, save the man.
VERNON HOWARD

39

True Contentment

WHEN NEWS GOT OUT that there was a new teacher who spoke with passion and great eloquence, the masses flocked to hear what he had to say. "Beyond the transitory, there is the lasting; beyond the fluctuating, there is the unchanging; beyond the peaks and valleys, there is a plateau. One day you will lay hold of it." When he had finished speaking, they questioned him. "Have you laid hold of it?"

**Nothing keeps one from being content
more than a mistaken idea of contentment.**

❮ ❮ ❮ ❮

*I have learned the secret of being content in any and every situation,
whether well fed or hungry, whether living in plenty or in want.*
PHILIPPIANS 4:12

The Oak and The Reed

❋ JEALOUS OF THE OAK, the reed said to herself, "I wish I would grow as tall, and as strong, and as firm, and as sturdy, and would be just as impressive as the oak." Then one day, a storm struck and the oak was swiftly uprooted. And the reed said to herself, "There is strength in weakness and beauty in frailty." And she no longer wished she were an oak.

**As fragile as they are,
reeds have no trouble withstanding a storm.**

❲ ❲ ❲ ❲

*God chooses as His instrument the humblest and
weakest of His creatures to fulfill Himself.*
GANDHI

Facing East

✸ WHEN DEPRESSION STRUCK, a man went to see the neighborhood psychiatrist who, to correct the imbalance, was quick to prescribe drugs. This stabilized his emotional states somewhat, but still he was deeply troubled, and so went to see the Master. After a brief exchange, the Master understood that the man felt as though he were being punished. "Why me?" he cried. When he deemed it appropriate, the Master, intervened. "Why not you?" At that, the man stopped. He didn't know how to respond. Sensing an opening, the Master added, "Can one see the sunrise while facing west?" "No," the man replied, "only while facing east." "The same holds true for you," said the Master. "Turn things around until you are facing east. Then you will see that you are not being punished, but are punishing yourself."

❰ ❰ ❰ ❰

By oneself is wrong done; by oneself one suffers.
SIDDHARTHA GAUTAMA

Lost in Thought

❀ A YOUNG MAN WENT to see the Master. Even before he opened his mouth, the Master detected a look of embarrassment and shame. "I see you are lost in thought," he said. "We will talk when I return. Meanwhile, be good enough to look after my roommate." The Master picked up a basket, removed the lid, pulled out a venomous snake, and handed it to the young man by the tail. "I will be gone for a short while," he said. "Give her your full attention; otherwise, she will strike." The young man obeyed, and instantly, his mind went silent. Not long after, the Master returned. "At last mind is defeated, and sorrow, vanquished with it," he said. The young man returned the snake, thanked the Master profusely, and left with a grin.

**When one looks with full attention,
the mind goes silent. Then there is great joy.**

☾ ☾ ☾ ☾

*Look to God that you may be radiant with joy
and your faces may not blush for shame.*
PSALM 34:6

43

Free of 'My'

✻ WHEN THE HUSBAND LOST his temper, his wife insisted that he go for counseling to better deal with his emotional outbursts. He refused to go for help, and things gradually worsened. Finally, in a desperate attempt to save his marriage, he opened up to an old friend. The friend listened as he shared his story. "I was never like this," he explained. "I used to be so relaxed and poised; what's happening to me?" "Nothing of any consequence," the friend replied. At that, the man grew angry. "What kind of friend are you?" he shouted. "Are my emotional outbursts of no concern to you?" "None whatsoever," replied the friend." "What concerns me is this word 'my.'"

Emotional storms happen to you.
They do not belong to you.

☾ ☾ ☾ ☾

One who abandons all desires, and becomes free from longing
and the feeling of 'I' and 'my,' attains peace.
BHAGAVAD GITA

The Puppet

✸ WHEN HE REALIZED HIS SORRY STATE, the puppet sought to free himself. He waited until his owner left the room, took a pair of scissors, and straightway began cutting his strings. He first cut the string that controlled his right arm, then the one that controlled his left arm. He cut the string that controlled his right leg, then the one that controlled his left leg. In just a short while, he cut every last string but one. Then he thought to himself, "If I cut this final string, I will no longer be a puppet, but a man." Suddenly, his mind was flooded with memories. He recalled his best performances, the elaborate sets, the time in the spotlight, the standing ovations, the choice wardrobes, and the resounding applause. He visited memory after memory until he could no longer go through with it, then he anxiously set about repairing his strings.

Freedom is to no longer compulsively visit the past.

❰ ❰ ❰ ❰

No one who sets a hand to the plow and looks to
what was left behind is fit for the kingdom of God.
LUKE 9:62

Questions and Answers

✺ THE MASTER OFTEN SPOKE of the value of questions. "More interesting are questions than answers," she would say. But this was always met with resistance by one of the group who insisted that answers always be given. The Master then responded, "There are some who dole out answers, who have not sufficiently struggled with the questions. And there are those who have struggled with the questions who have the good sense to know that another may find altogether different answers."

❨ ❨ ❨ ❨

It is better to know some of the questions than all of the answers.
JAMES THURBER

The Defense

✸ A LARGE SUM OF MONEY was stolen and later returned. When the owner saw that the money had been returned, he took a small portion and hired an off-duty cop to track down whoever returned it. After asking a few routine questions, the officer found his way to the doorstep of a man who perfectly fit the profile. He knocked on the door. "Who is it?" the man replied. "It's the police." The man slowly walked toward the door and opened it. There stood the off-duty cop, together with his partner. "It wasn't me," he cried. "I didn't do it." "You didn't do what?" they asked. "Whatever you think I did," said the man. "I didn't do it." "So then you're not responsible?" "No I'm not responsible. I had nothing to do with it," said the man. "My mistake," said the officer. "Sorry for the disturbance." The man closed the door as the two officers walked away. "And to think we almost gave the reward money to the wrong man."

**Be slow to come to your defense
and you'll be richly rewarded.**

❨ ❨ ❨ ❨

*Make up your minds not to prepare beforehand to defend yourselves;
for I will give you utterance and wisdom which none of
your opponents will be able to resist or refute.*
LUKE 21:14

The Concert

❀ A COUPLE WAS GIVEN tickets to a concert, which they put away for safekeeping. As the weeks rolled by, they read the reviews in anticipation and looked forward to going themselves. One night while out on the town, they overheard a man talking about the show. They watched how his face lit up as he described in detail the marvelous music. "We plan on going tomorrow," they said excitedly. "You are mistaken," said the man. "The concert is going on now." At that, they hurried home and pulled out their tickets. It was just as the man had said. The concert was going on and they were missing it.

**The great teachers insist that eternal life is now.
Are you missing it?**

❨ ❨ ❨ ❨

*When you see that God acts through you at every moment,
in every movement of mind or body, you attain true freedom.
When you realize the truth, and cling to nothing
in the world, you enter eternal life.*
UPANISHADS

Good Counsel

✸ A YOUNG MAN CAME to the Master deeply troubled about the future. The Master listened patiently. Then, taking a book off the shelf, she opened it and gave it to the young man to read.

Therefore, I tell you do not be anxious about your life, what you shall eat, or what you shall drink, nor about your body, what you shall put on. Is not life more than food, and the body more than clothing? Look at the birds of the air; they neither sow nor reap nor gather into barns, and yet your heavenly Father feeds them. Are you not of more value than they? And which of you by being anxious could add one cubit to his span of life?…therefore, do not be anxious about tomorrow, for tomorrow will be anxious for itself. Let the day's own trouble be sufficient for the day.

When the boy read the passage, he immediately calmed down. The Master turned to him and said, "If you have the tabloids in one hand, you must have the Scriptures in the other."

❆ ❆ ❆ ❆

Better than a thousand meaningless words is one sensible word if hearing it one becomes peaceful.
SIDDHARTHA GAUTAMA

In the Interest of Peace

� A GROUP OF MEN GOT TOGETHER, who called themselves
P.O.W. When a man asked what it stood for, they proudly remarked
that the acronym stood for "Peacemakers of the World." "That sounds
impressive," he said. "What exactly do you do?" "Well, at the moment,
we are raising money to buy more sophisticated weapons." "Weapons?" asked the man. "That is correct. We are one-hundred percent
committed to fighting the enemy in the interest of peace."

**True peacemakers are armed not
with weapons, but understanding.**

☾ ☾ ☾ ☾

*The sage, when employed, becomes the Head of all the
Officers [of government]; and in his greatest
regulations he employs no violent measures.*
LAO-TSU

True Success

✺ AS A KIND GESTURE, a troubadour gave a woman a beautiful poem and invited her for a drink. Although she found it both romantic and sweet, she declined his offer, saying, "You're not my type. You simply don't have any of the qualities I look for." Seeing that he wasn't the slightest bit put off by her rejection, she turned to him and said, "On second thought, why don't we have that drink?"

**The world values only measurable success
until encountering true success.**

❨ ❨ ❨ ❨

*If you want to succeed you should strike out on new paths,
rather than travel the worn paths of accepted success.*
JOHN D. ROCKEFELLER

What Is Most Frightening?

⊛ THE MASTER CONSISTENTLY taught that God is love, and yet in the same breath, she spoke of the "great and terrible day of the Lord." When asked by her pupils if this wasn't a contradiction, she replied, "What is more frightening than love?"

To love you must risk it all; you must reveal yourself as you are. Tell me, what is more frightening than love?

☾ ☾ ☾ ☾

Love takes off masks that we fear we cannot live without and know we cannot live within.
JAMES BALDWIN

The Best Education

✴ THE MASTER TAUGHT extensively about the value of travel. "Travel," he said, "is undeniably the best education." He justified his remark in this way: "A fish in a small tank grows only as much as the tank will allow, but if it is put into greater waters, it will grow to a greater size. So it is with one who explores the different cultures of the world—his vision is broadened by his vast experience."

❨ ❨ ❨ ❨

To travel is to discover that everyone is wrong about other countries.
ALDOUS HUXLEY

Unite or Divide?

⊛ THE MASTER WAS ASKED THIS QUESTION: "Does the truth unite or divide?" "Both," she answered. "Under one roof, the truth unites everyone who does not cherish too highly their opinions." To make her point, she told the story of a group of students who got together to discuss whether God was male or female. Just five minutes into the debate, they were intense and divided. Some claimed God was 'Father.' Some said God was 'Mother.' The Master replied that God was Father, Mother, and neither, and they came together as one.

**The truth is always just beyond
what you think you know.**

❨ ❨ ❨ ❨

Don't keep searching for the truth, just let go of your opinions.
SENG TS'AN

The Essence of Spirituality

✪ THE MASTER TALKED OFTEN about the essence of spirituality. He taught that if people understood the essence of spirituality, wars would cease, abuse would vanish, and laughter and joy would abound. Finally, the question came. "What is spirituality?" they asked. His response: "To weep with those who weep and to rejoice with those who rejoice."

**Sensitivity and universality
are the clearest signs of true spirituality.**

❰ ❰ ❰ ❰

*When a person responds to the joys and sorrows of others as if they
were his own, he has attained the highest state of spiritual union.*
BHAGAVAD GITA

The Desert

❀ WHILE ON A JOURNEY, a man lost his way and ended up traveling through the desert. Despite the conditions, he traveled for a time but eventually was overcome by blazing heat and desert storms. Exhausted, he lay defeated on the ground, his muscles cramped, his lips chapped and dry. "What have I done to suffer this cruel fate?" he wondered. Shortly after, the man died of thirst. His only impulse was to reproach God. "Why did you leave me to die in the desert? Why did you abandon me to the blazing heat and not give me water?" And God replied— "You never asked."

You are in the desert. Have you asked for water?

❰ ❰ ❰ ❰

If you knew the gift of God and who it is that asks
you for a drink, you would have asked him
and he would have given you living water.
JOHN 4:10

On the Side of Life

✳ A MAN WAS CONVICTED OF MURDER and awaited sentencing. Seized by fear, he reverted to the faith of his childhood and mumbled to himself a silent prayer. When the judge returned, she sentenced the man to life in prison without parole. Outraged, the crowd became vocal. "This man should have been given the death penalty, then Divine justice would have prevailed." When the judge heard this, she immediately spoke up. "Is God not on the side of life?" she asked. "Yes, and this man takes lives," said the crowd. "Regrettably," said the judge, "so do we."

**The problem with standing with one group
is you've got to stand against others.**

☾ ☾ ☾ ☾

If you want to realize the truth, don't be for or against.
SENG TS'AN

The Guide

✹ A GROUP OF MEN DECIDED to go mountain climbing and so requested a guide. Just moments later, out stepped a woman with a walking stick. "Is she blind?" they asked. "Only physically," said the ranger, "otherwise she has the sight of an eagle." Puzzled, they accepted the guide and began walking along the stony path. When they had gone just a few miles, one of the men spoke up. "Look, a shortcut!" "There are no shortcuts," replied the guide. And so they continued on. Then said a second man, "Look, a smoother path, which appears to lead up." The guide kept walking. "The path only appears to lead up," she said. And so they continued on their way. Then said a third man, "Look, the clouds are dark and threatening." "They are not real," said the guide. And so they continued on. Then said a fourth man, "Look over there. The rocks are falling." "You are in no danger," she replied. And they continued on. Then said a fifth man, "Look in the shadows. There are ravenous wolves." And they were deeply afraid. And the guide consoled them. "Fear is your only obstacle. Overcome it and you will see."

☾ ☾ ☾ ☾

Obstacles are like wild animals. They are cowards but they will bluff you if they can. If they see you are afraid of them… they are liable to spring upon you; but if you look them squarely in the eye, they will slink out of sight.
ORISON SWETT MARDEN

Just Two Kinds

✺ THE MASTER OFTEN WARNED his disciples that piety, fidelity, and religious fervor could mean their demise. These practices, he maintained, were known to harden men's hearts, and by them many were damned. Local church officials protested on the basis that the Master was corrupting the youth and teaching blasphemy. Finally, they gave this ultimatum: "Instruct them rightly using the Scriptures or we shall take further action." "I did," he replied. "Have you not read The Prodigal Son?"

Of people, there are only two kinds: those who insist that they themselves are good, and those who boast that God is.

❨ ❨ ❨ ❨

Good teacher, what must I do to inherit eternal life?"
Jesus answered him, "Why do you call me good?
No one is good but God alone."
MARK 10:17–18

Solving Problems

✹ WHEN A DISTANT PLANET became over populated, its inhabitants searched the galaxy for a new residence. When it was suggested
they travel to Earth, one spoke up. "But we have never been to Earth.
Suppose there is no oxygen or water, how then will we live?" "You
raise a valid point," the group replied. "Let us organize a committee
and find a solution."

**The problem of most people is that they
are busy solving problems that don't exist.**

❨ ❨ ❨ ❨

*This is what enlightenment is all about:
a deep understanding that there is no problem.
Then, with no problem to solve, what will you do?
Immediately you start living.*
OSHO

The Prize Pupil

❀ WHEN THE PRIZE PUPIL went to see the Master about leaving the monastery, the Master didn't hesitate, but insisted that he was not ready. When asked how long it would be until he was ready, the Master was silent and invited the boy to join him on his walk. Together the two of them made their way until stopping before a trickling waterfall. The Master then turned to the boy and said, "As long as it takes for the water to enter the rock." Realizing this was his answer, the boy nodded in deep humility. The Master then sought to console him. "There is a blessing and a curse in being the prize pupil," he said. "Often you take hold of the truth sooner than it takes hold of you."

❆ ❆ ❆ ❆

Some people will never learn anything...
because they understand everything too soon.
ALEXANDER POPE

The Boy King

✸ THE BOY WAS MADE KING when he came of age. He was provided with a scepter, a crown, a royal robe, faithful subjects, and wise counselors. The kingdom was left in his care to rule. Not long after, the boy king was overthrown, and he and his subjects found themselves imprisoned. There the king lamented and grieved his loss. Sensing he was troubled, one of the wise counselors interrupted. "Pardon me, your Grace, but may I make a suggestion?" "Speak," said the king. "Suppose for a moment that you were not who you think you are, would you then need a kingdom?" "Well, no," replied the king. "Would you need a crown or a royal robe?" "I suppose not," said the king. "How about a scepter or faithful subjects?" "I would need neither," said the king. "What are you suggesting?" The wise counselor leaned toward the king and whispered, "Lose the title."

Who you think you are and what you think you need are closely connected.

❬ ❬ ❬ ❬

If we liberate our souls from our petty selves, wish no ill to others,
and become clear as a crystal diamond reflecting the light of truth,
what a radiant picture will appear in us mirroring things as they are,
without the admixture of burning desires, without the distortion
of erroneous illusion, without the agitation of clinging and unrest.
SIDDHARTHA GAUTAMA

A Class in Mindfulness

❀ WHEN ASKED WHAT CLASSES were being offered at the college, the registrar announced that they were offering classes in Yoga, Pilates, Tai Chi, Chi Gong, and a class in mindfulness. Intrigued, some students enrolled in the class in mindfulness and faithfully attended each session. They completed the course, praised the instructor, and were heading home when suddenly they were pulled over by the local police. "Are you aware that you just went through a red light?" "We did?" they responded. "Sorry officer, I guess we weren't paying attention."

You only really learn what you practice.

☾ ☾ ☾ ☾

Learning is a good thing; but it availeth not.
True wisdom can be acquired by practice only.
SIDDHARTHA GAUTAMA

The Book

✹ ANXIOUS AND RESTLESS, A YOUNG executive sought out a master, who quietly listened as he spoke. When he finished, the Master handed him a book. "Read only the first page and come tomorrow at the same time." The young executive did as he was instructed and returned the following day. "How much of it have you read?" "A single page," said the executive. "Very well, return tomorrow," said the Master. "Only this time, once you have read a page, I want you to tear it out." The young executive obeyed, and when he had read the next page, he tore it out and returned the following day. This kept up for a number of weeks. "How do you think the book will end?" the Master asked. "I don't know," the executive replied. "I've one more chapter to read." The Master then asked for the book, opened it, and proceeded to tear out the final chapter. "What have you done? The book has but a single page?" "And you have but this present moment."

**What would life be like if you had no remembrance
of the past and no thought for tomorrow?
Answer: Eternity.**

❨ ❨ ❨ ❨

*One instant is eternity; eternity is the now. When you see
through this one instant, you see through the one who sees.*
WU-MEN

If You Remain

⊛ THE MASTER LED HER disciples into the forest and sat them down before an enormous tree. "If you abide for a moment, you are the leaves," she said, "and go wherever the wind takes you. If you sit for a time, you are the branches and bend the way the wind blows. If you dwell for a while, you are the trunk and lean ever so slightly, but if you remain, you are the roots, secure no matter what the season."

☾ ☾ ☾ ☾

Whoever does the will of God remains forever.
1 JOHN 2:17

The Sabbatical

✳ WHEN THE PRIEST MENTIONED that he would be taking a sabbatical, some parishioners inquired as to the date of his return. "When the time is right," replied the priest. "Are you going far?" they asked. "Yes, quite far," said the priest. "As far as Rome?" they asked. "Somewhere even more remote," said the priest. "To the Holy Land?" "A place still more distant," said the priest. "How soon are you leaving?" "I just left."

Near is the place that is worlds away.

☾ ☾ ☾ ☾

Without going outside his door,
one understands (all that takes place) under the sky;
without looking out from his window,
one sees the Tao of Heaven…
LAO-TSU

A Teacher and a Master

✻ A DISPUTE AROSE AS TO WHAT the difference was between a teacher and a master. Some argued that there was no difference whatsoever, that it was largely a question of semantics. Others perceived the difference as having more to do with status or level of expertise. The Master settled the dispute, saying, "The heart of the matter is this: The teacher instructs only by his words, the Master instructs even by his silence."

☾ ☾ ☾ ☾

The sage manages affairs without doing anything,
and conveys his instructions without the use of speech.
LAO-TSU

Without Power

A MAN DECIDED TO BRING his family and extended family to a rustic cottage for the holidays. Together they put up the tree, hung the tinsel, and decorated the cabin with lights. Not long after, a neighbor noticed the abundance of light and came and knocked on the door. "I have family up for the weekend," he said, "but am without power." Feeling pity, the man agreed to share what was his. The neighbor likewise put up his tree, hung the tinsel, and decorated his cabin with lights. Finally, the man plugged in, and within seconds, the lights dimmed.

Cut loose from needy neighbors
and your light will again burn brightly.

Most people recognize energy suckers but still engage
with them out of guilt or a sense of duty.
TONYA SOMERS

The Shell

❊ WHEN CIRCUMSTANCES FORCED the young man to move inland, the father thought fit to take his son scuba diving. For hours on end the two of them explored the deep sea and all it had to offer. When their time had ended, the son turned to his father and said, "I will never forget this moment. I will treasure it forever." The father smiled, put his hand on his son's shoulder, and again disappeared beneath the deep blue waters. Moments later, he produced a brightly colored shell from the ocean floor and gave it to his son. "If ever you feel lonely or far off, just listen, and you will hear the sea."

**Should circumstances force you inland,
remember what you've received from the Father.**

☾ ☾ ☾ ☾

*Do not be afraid, little flock, for your Father
has been pleased to give you the kingdom.*
LUKE 12:32

A Fondness for Criticism

✸ WHEN THE MASTER WAS ASKED, "What keeps the masses from enlightenment?" He replied, "Mostly, a fondness for criticism." When asked what he meant, he told the story of an athlete who got up somewhat dazed and scored a goal for the opposing team. The criticisms escalated. "Did you see what he did?" said one. "I can't believe my eyes," said another. "What a world class fool," said a third. "That is what keeps them from enlightenment." He added, "They level criticism after criticism, all the while scoring points for the opposing team."

❰ ❰ ❰ ❰

I have yet to meet the man who can see
his own faults and censure himself.
CONFUCIUS

Nobody Home

❀ ONE DAY GOD WENT IN SEARCH of an earthly residence. He stopped at the first home, but because of a sign that read NO VACANCY, God shook the dust from His feet and quietly moved on. He approached a second home and knocked on the door. At once a resident answered, who offered to share the sizable space, but God declined the resident's offer and peacefully pressed on. Then God came to a third house and gave a knock at the door, but no answer. He peered through the window; no light was on. He opened the door; no one was present. Instantly He entered and hung His hat and coat.

**God will settle in your house
when you no longer reside there.**

☾ ☾ ☾ ☾

There is not room in the house for two I's.
RUMI

The Ladder

✺ THE COUNTENANCE OF ONE WOMAN grew so bright that everyone in the village referred to her as "the friend of God." Rumor had it that in addition to being a woman of prayer, she had in her possession a mystical ladder that was said to reach heaven itself. When the ruler got wind of this, he reasoned that if there were such a ladder it should belong to him. So he gave orders that the ladder be found and brought to him at once. The authorities obeyed the command and brought both the woman and the ladder before him. The ruler looked at the woman, then at the ladder. "It has no rungs!" he cried. "What good is a ladder without rungs? Explain yourself!" The friend of God spoke: "The value of the ladder lies not in its ability to reach heaven, but to recall our inability to do so."

**The value of your prayer lies not in your method,
but in the realization that no method will suffice.**

❨ ❨ ❨ ❨

*Remind those who tell you otherwise that
Love comes to you of its own accord,
and the yearning for it cannot be learned in any school.*
RUMI

How Many Sides?

❀ THE MASTER GATHERED HIS disciples beneath a tree and posed this question: "Tell me, how many sides does a coconut have?" Not knowing how to answer, the disciples fell silent. He asked a second time. "How many sides are there to a coconut?" "None," they replied. "A coconut has no sides." At that, the Master took one in hand, drew a knife from his belt, and split it in two. "Wrong," he exclaimed, "it has two, an inside and an outside."

**When you think of passing judgment,
consider this; everything has at least two sides.**

❨ ❨ ❨ ❨

*Not as man sees does God see,
because man sees the appearance
but the Lord looks into the heart.*
1 SAMUEL 16:7

The Widow

✹ WHEN THE WIDOW LOST her husband of twenty years, she grieved inconsolably day and night. Whenever in public, she hid her tear stained cheeks behind a lace vale and wore black as a sign of mourning. Many praised what they called her "undying devotion to her dead husband." Months passed, and still the sobs didn't let up. One villager then said to another, "Have you ever in your life witnessed such enduring love?" "Yes," the other replied, "but never such fondness for misery."

❨ ❨ ❨ ❨

There is only one way of being cured of sadness,
and that is to dislike being sad.
LOUIS EVELY

The Monk's Robe

❋ WHEN THE MONK DISCOVERED he was to be awarded the Nobel Peace Prize, he immediately began the hunt for his best robe. Not finding it, he sought out an elder and disclosed his dilemma. "I am expected to receive a medal, but have no robe to wear." "That is the least of your problems," replied the elder. "What do you mean?" asked the monk. "I mean that there is also no one to wear the robe."

Selflessness is a virtue only when taken literally.

❨ ❨ ❨ ❨

I am He who is; you are she who is not.
THE DIALOGUES OF ST. CATHERINE OF SIENA

Open Them

✸ IN AN EFFORT TO BRING AN END to domestic violence, the Master spoke to the people, "It is good sense to be slow to anger, and it is your glory to overlook an offense." When She had said this, an activist stood up and fired a rebuttal. "That's not realistic," exclaimed the activist. "When we are treated unfairly, do you expect us to just close our eyes?" "No," said the Master, "I expect you to open them."

Those asleep see anger as a veritable option.
Those awake see it as the opposition.

❨ ❨ ❨ ❨

A person whose mind is unperturbed by sorrow, who does not
crave pleasures, and who is completely free from attachment, fear,
and anger, is called an enlightened sage of steady intellect.
BHAGAVAD GITA

The Collision

❀ A FOREIGN SHIP SET OUT on a voyage to a new land. With their beloved captain at the helm, the crew sought safe passage across the icy waters. But, being the stranger that he was, the captain's unfamiliarity with glaciers led to a collision with an iceberg, and subsequently the boat sank.

**Continue on the surface and
you'll collide with what's beneath.**

☾ ☾ ☾ ☾

*Man's task is to become conscious of the contents
that press upward from the unconscious.*
CARL GUSTAV JUNG

The Statue

✺ WHEN THE EFFORTS of a religious leader brought peace to their war-torn country, the inhabitants sought to immortalize her. They invited her to a banquet, presented her with a title, and erected a bronze statue in her honor. When she discovered that this had been done, immediately, she requested that the monument be torn down. "For what reason?" they asked. She answered, "Put me on a pedestal, and I shall become even more difficult to imitate."

Woe to you who are awed by heroes but not inspired.

☾ ☾ ☾ ☾

It is the capacity not to worship buddhas but to become a Buddha;
not to follow others but to develop the awareness within that
brings a quality of light and love to all that we do.
OSHO

The Teacher

✸ WHEN THE BELL RANG, the students hastily made their way to the classroom. They arrived and found the room empty with not so much as a desk. Bewildered, they looked about then recalled that class was to be held in the chapel. Not wanting to be late, they hurried to the chapel where they discovered several rows of chairs and a large wooden desk. Upon it: an attendance book, a stapler, a coffee mug filled with pens and pencils, even an apple, but the teacher was nowhere in sight.

The Teacher who is out of sight is not out of reach.

❨ ❨ ❨ ❨

It is written in the prophets, 'And they shall all be taught by God.'
JOHN 6:45

The Anxious Young Man

THE MASTER WAS INVITED to speak to the youth on the topic of growth and change. When he had finished, a young man eagerly approached him and asked, "Master, how does one change?" He took one look at the anxious young man and said, "Gradually."

❨ ❨ ❨ ❨

Perfection is attained by slow degrees; it requires the hand of time.
VOLTAIRE

The Brain Chip

✴ AN AWARD-WINNING SCIENTIST built a robot and equipped it with intelligence by adding a brain chip. Unlike the inferior technology of previous scientists that programmed robots to perform daily tasks and learn from experience, this chip gave the robot access to the creator's own brain. When a colleague asked what made such breakthroughs possible, he replied, "The absence of all programming."

**Why try to read the mind of God
when you can possess it?**

❨ ❨ ❨ ❨

"Who has known the mind of the Lord that he may instruct him?"
But we have the mind of Christ.
1 CORINTHIANS 2:16

Already Lost

⊛ A PROPHET WHO WARNED of impending disaster visited the king. "What am I to do?" asked the king. "Withdraw from battle," advised the prophet. "Will not such an act be perceived as cowardice? If I withdraw from battle what will people think?" "If that is your worry," replied the prophet, "then you've already lost the battle."

☾ ☾ ☾ ☾

How can you believe when you accept praise from one another, and do not seek the praise that comes from the only God.
JOHN 5:44

The Liberating Truth

❋ WHEN A YOUNG MAN WENT to see the Master, he noticed a plaque on the wall. It read:

What you do,
Why you do,
You need not do.

When asked what the words meant, the Master replied, "To most they mean absolutely nothing." "And to you?" the young man asked. "To me," replied the Master "it is the most liberating truth."

The prisoner who does not recognize
his cell cannot recognize the key.

❨ ❨ ❨ ❨

All wrongdoing arises because of mind.
If mind is transformed can wrongdoing remain?
SIDDHARTHA GAUTAMA

The Birthright

✳ WHILE PLAYING IN THE FOREST, a cub was encircled by a vicious group of jackals. When the mother saw this, she gave a loud roar, which sent the aggressors away in terror. "What was that?" asked the cub. "That was a demonstration of authority," replied the mother. "Do I have authority?" asked the cub. "Yes, it is your birthright, as king of the jungle." "My birthright?" "That is correct. When you discover who you are, the roar will come. Then you are no longer a cub, but a lion."

❰ ❰ ❰ ❰

I have given you authority to trample on snakes and scorpions and
to overcome all the power of the enemy; nothing will harm you.
LUKE 10:19

The Prisoner

❀ A MAN WAS FALSELY ACCUSED of murder and brought to trial. After the proceedings, he was found guilty and received life in prison without parole. For years, he kept to himself and left his cell only to receive the occasional visitor. One day an inmate approached him. "Don't you get tired of the same four walls?" "Walls?" he replied. "I hardly notice them."

No cell can imprison the man who
is not restricted by his own mind.

☾ ☾ ☾ ☾

I know but one freedom, and that is the freedom of the mind.
ANTOINE DE SAINT-EXUPERY

A New Home

✹ A WOMAN CAME TO SEE the Master about a haunting past. Aware that she had just purchased a new home, the Master thought to ask her how she was getting along and if she had recently given any thought to returning to her former house. "Certainly not," replied the woman. "Why is that?" asked the Master. "Because the old house did not have the convenience nor the space nor the worth of the new one." The Master then turned to the woman and asked, "Then why do you return to a haunting past?"

It makes as much sense to return to painful past thoughts as it does to vacate a beautiful new home.

☾ ☾ ☾ ☾

Forget the former things; do not dwell on the past.
See I am doing a new thing!
Now it springs up; do you not perceive it?
ISAIAH 43:18–19

Not the Reality

ALTHOUGH THE WOMAN WAS THOUGHT to be a saint, she was criticized for rarely speaking to her disciples of God. When confronted by her peers about the matter, she replied, "If I spoke to you of food, would you be nourished?" "No," they answered. "If I told you of sunlight, would you be warmed?" "Not in the least," said they. "Then what does it serve to speak of God? Words are not the reality."

Knowledge of God cannot make you a saint any more than facts about sunlight can warm you.

❈ ❈ ❈ ❈

All apprehension and knowledge of supernatural things cannot help us to love God so much as the least act of living faith and hope made in detachment from all things.
ST. JOHN OF THE CROSS

The Three-Story Home

❀ ALL OF HIS EARTHLY LIFE, the young man resided in a three-story home. Although most of his time was spent on the middle floor, every so often he would venture to the basement. He was charmed by the dark unfurnished space, and he embraced it as a place of secrecy and adventure, of thrill and mischief. As time passed, the allures of the lower level beguiled him, and soon it became his habitual dwelling. Seldom did he visit the middle floor and never did he go to the upper floor. Then one day out of the blue, the idea came to journey upstairs. So accustomed was he to the dark that even the middle floor now seemed bright to him. In time, he adjusted and eventually made his way to the upper floor, which was fully furnished and complete with every comfort. He left the basement and settled anew.

The level of your mind is the level of your habitation.

❨ ❨ ❨ ❨

Whatever is true, whatever is noble, whatever is right,
whatever is pure, whatever is lovely, whatever is admirable—
if anything is excellent or praiseworthy—think about such things.
PHILIPPIANS 4:8

The Flower Doesn't Doubt

✸ WHILE THE MASTER WAS GARDENING, one of the disciples came and asked how long it would take for him to end a destructive habit. Her reply, "As long as it takes to break all attachment and association with the habit, and not a minute more." She then watered and fertilized the rose bed. "Tell me," she asked. "Why doesn't the flower die?" "Because all the water and nourishment the flower requires is here in the rose bed," replied the disciple. "So is all the grace that you desire in this present moment," said the Master. "The only difference is the flower doesn't doubt."

❨ ❨ ❨ ❨

Whatever you ask for in prayer,
believe that you have received it, and it will be yours.
MARK 11:24

The Affair

✹ A COUPLE GOT MARRIED and settled down to enjoy their new life together. But the economy changed, money grew tight, and the husband was forced to get a second job. For a time, things went well. But later, his frequent absence led to her having an affair. Not wanting to conceal her shame, she confessed her infidelity outright. At once, the husband's eyes filled with tears. He left the house to wander the streets and moments later found himself seated on the steps of a nearby church. He got up, went inside, and fell before an enormous crucifix. "I have every right to divorce her," he said. "And," replied God, "you have every reason to forgive."

Don't give up on people. Rather, give up on your belief that they must meet your expectations.

❨ ❨ ❨ ❨

If you cannot be as you would like,
how can you expect others to be as you would like?
THOMAS A. KEMPIS

Prayer of the 'I'

✸ AFTER ATTENDING PART of the Master's retreat, a young man felt compelled to write a letter. "I have heard the expression 'prayer of the heart,' but exactly what did you mean by 'prayer of the eye'?" The Master wrote back, "Not the *eye*, but the *I*."

The "I" is the treasure hidden in the field, the lost drachma, and the pearl of great price. To know it is to know one's innermost Self as one with Being.

☾ ☾ ☾ ☾

The Supreme Being is the source of all lights.
He is said to be beyond darkness of ignorance.
He is the Self-knowledge, the object of Self-knowledge,
and seated in the inner psyche as consciousness.
BHAGAVAD GITA

Extinguishing the False Self

✹ THE MASTER TOOK A HATCHET and his disciples and went into the woods. Together they worked to clear a spot, gather twigs, and start a small fire. Seated about the fire, they sang songs, told stories, and danced well into evening. When it came time for the merriment to end, the Master instructed the fire be put out. Without water or sand, the disciples worked against the flames in the only way they knew how, by no longer adding twigs to the fire.

**Apply this very same logic,
and you will one day extinguish the false self.**

☾ ☾ ☾ ☾

When nothing is done, nothing is left undone.
LAO-TSU

Pure Consciousness

✺ A PHILOSOPHER, A PSYCHOLOGIST, and a mystic got together to discuss their differences and to better understand one another. The philosopher spoke first. "A person is an individual substance with a rational nature. Thus, the philosopher's words are fitting, 'I think, therefore, I am.'" The psychologist replied, "A person is an emotional being with rational capability. Thus, it is rightly said that, 'Humans are governed more by their feelings than by reason.'" Finally, the mystic spoke. "A person is pure consciousness. He is nether the thinker, nor the feeler. Thus it is aptly put, 'He is awareness itself.'" At that, the others were enlightened.

How many acquainted with thoughts and feelings have had no contact with themselves?

☾ ☾ ☾ ☾

*The beginning of freedom is the realization that you are not
"the thinker." The moment you start watching the thinker,
a higher level of consciousness becomes activated.*
ECKHART TOLLE

Without Sin

⚙ THE MASTER POSED this question to the preacher, who professed to know the mind of God, "What is God's opinion of sinners?" "He loves the sinner, but hates the sin," was the reply. "Isn't that a bit like loving the dish and hating the ingredients?" the Master asked. "How so?" asked the preacher. "Because the dish would not be the same without all the ingredients, and neither would man be man without sin."

**No matter how bright it gets,
there is still darkness in the center of a flame.**

❨ ❨ ❨ ❨

*Jesus would not trust himself to them because he knew them all,
and did not need anyone to testify about human nature.
He himself understood it well.*
JOHN 3:24–25

The Builder and the Townhouse

�֍ ALMOST OVERNIGHT, A BUILDER put up townhouses in a middleclass neighborhood. He laid the flooring, finished the drywall, hung the fixtures, and furnished the model exquisitely. When a well-known movie producer showed up with a camera crew, he did not hesitate but straightaway took him to see the unit. "I'll take it." "You won't be disappointed," said the builder. Without warning, the producer then hurled his foot through the wall. "You're right about that," he said. "Given the substandard quality, this house should collapse better than any."

**When words dismantle your ego, consider this:
they come not from spite, but from Truth.**

❨ ❨ ❨ ❨

*You say, 'I am rich;
I have acquired wealth and do not need a thing.'
But you do not realize that you are wretched,
pitiful, poor, blind and naked.*
REVELATION 3:17

Watching Boats

✹ EVERY SUNDAY THE FATHER LOVED to sit with his son on the shore and watch the boats. If ever the son fancied one, eagerly he would tug at his father's sleeve. "Let's go aboard that one," he insisted. "That one will take you further from land," the father replied. Moments passed and so did the next attractive boat. "That one!" cried the son. "Let's go aboard that one." "That one likewise will take you away from shore," replied the father. "Will not all boats take us from the shore?" asked the boy. "Yes, that is their nature," said the father. "That is why, rather than climb aboard, we happily watch them go by."

**Meditation is sitting on the shore of God's love,
happily watching thoughts go by.**

☾ ☾ ☾ ☾

*The entity that says, "I would like to have marvelous experiences,
therefore I must force my brain to be quiet," will never do it.
But if you begin to inquire, observe, listen to all the moments
of thought, its conditionings, its pursuits, its fears, its pleasures,
watch how the brain operates, then you will see that
the brain becomes extraordinarily quiet.*
J. KRISHNAMURTI

Who Do You Revere?

✴ A YOUNG MAN WAS MINDING his own affairs when he was approached by a large group of people. "Who do you revere?" they asked. "The Risen One or the Enlightened One?" "Who should I revere?" asked the man. "Well, the Risen One, of course, who has freed you from the bonds of sin and death." "Well," said the man, "I shall not be ungrateful. I shall indeed revere the Risen One." Not long after, he was approached a second time, again by a large group of people. "Who do you revere?" they asked. "The Enlightened One or the Risen One?" "Who should I revere?" he asked. "Well, the Enlightened One, of course, who has freed you from delusion and suffering." "Well," said the man, "I shall not be ungrateful. I shall indeed revere the Enlightened One."

Then came a third group. "Who do you revere?" they asked. "Well," said the man, "I revere the Risen One, who frees me from sin and death, and the Enlightened One, who delivers me from ignorance and suffering."

☾ ☾ ☾ ☾

Many will come from the east and the west,
and will take their places at the feast with Abraham,
Isaac and Jacob in the kingdom of heaven.
MATTHEW 8:11

Past Thought

❋ THE MASTER OFTEN SAID that if getting a student to think was an accomplishment, getting one past thought was a true victory. When asked what he meant, he countered with this question. "Were you to build a house, you would first need a location, then an architect, skilled laborers, then raw materials, a method of going about it, a time to begin, and a deadline in which to finish. Now, were you to build a sound mind or a good heart, how then would you proceed?"

❨ ❨ ❨ ❨

Between living and dreaming there is a third thing, guess it.
ANTONIO MACHADO

The Five-Year Plan

✴ WHILE ENGAGED IN SPIRITUAL READING, a young aspirant fell upon a passage in Scripture. Immediately he transcribed the passage and the very next day worked out a plan by which he would become a great saint. His plan included: spending more time in prayer, practicing detachment, occasional fasting, and an increased amount of spiritual reading. When the young aspirant had completed the details of his plan, he took it to show his spiritual director, who surprisingly tore it to bits. "What have you done?" shouted the young man. "That was my five-year plan to become a saint!" "Then you ought to thank me," replied the director. "I've saved you the trouble of waiting five years."

Ask not how you can plan for the future,
but rather how you can respond to this moment.

❨ ❨ ❨ ❨

In an acceptable time I have heard you,
and on the day of salvation I helped you.
Behold now is a very acceptable time,
now is the day of salvation.
2 CORINTHIANS 6:2

The Sculptor

✤ WHEN THE ASPIRANT PASSED all her time in meditation, she was duly criticized. "That is not the middle path," they said. And from then on, she set out to choose a craft that was both useful and contemplative. After several failed attempts, she found a perfect match and began chiseling beautiful and inspiring sculptures from blocks of ice. Before long, she became proficient and eventually opened a shop. Word spread quickly and the villagers came in droves, some out of curiosity, others out of devotion, and still others because they needed ice. Nevertheless, there for all to admire were spectacular sculptures: beautiful carvings of Christ and the Madonna, Sri Krishna and Buddha, Mohammed and Lao-Tsu, Gandhi, Mother Teresa, and various other saints and mystics. Finally one of the villagers spoke up, "All are exquisite, but what do they have in common?" The sculptor smiled and said, "All are ice!"

**As water takes on many forms,
God assumes many bodies.**

❨ ❨ ❨ ❨

*Christ plays in ten thousand places, lovely in limbs, and lovely
in eyes not his to the Father through the features of men's faces.*
GERARD MANLEY HOPKINS

The Creed

❀ ONCE UPON A TIME a Hindu, a Buddhist, a Moslem, a Jew, and a Christian combined efforts to compose a creed. After their time together, they came up with this: There are many guidelines but only one law. There are many persons but only one Self. There are many revelations but only one Truth. There are many religions but only one God. Understand this and you will merge with the way things are. From that day on, they grew in grace and wisdom and lived happily ever after.

The mystics agree. Why can't anyone else?

☾ ☾ ☾ ☾

I am in love with every church, and mosque,
and temple, and any kind of shrine;
because I know it is there that people say
the different names of the one God.
HAFIZ

True Evangelization

✸ A MISSIONARY, HAVING GREAT RESPECT for other cultures, set out to evangelize aborigines. He taught them to read and write and left them with a copy of Scripture before he was abruptly called away. Years later, he returned to see what progress, if any, had been made. With tears in his eyes, he watched as the aborigines danced, sang songs, read from the sacred text, and took turns prostrating before one another, then he returned to the mainland to awaken his own people.

What is the good news, but the inconceivable truth of your own divine nature?

❨ ❨ ❨ ❨

Is it not written in your Law, I have said you are gods?
JOHN 10:34

The Shadow

WHEN ASKED BY HIS DISCIPLES how one arrives at perfection, the Master answered with a question: "Can a man travel in daylight without his shadow?" "No," the disciples responded. "So it is with perfection, no one truly arrives. With light there is always shadow."

☾ ☾ ☾ ☾

A good traveler has no fixed plans and is not intent upon arriving.
LAO-TSU

Spoken Plainly

❋ ONE DAY THE MASTER VANISHED, leaving no one to continue his legacy. So deceptively simple was his teaching that even his disciples misunderstood him. Out of the mass confusion emerged a variety of interpretations and schools, until one day the Master returned with what seemed to be a fresh teaching. When asked for an explanation, he replied, "Last time I spoke to you in parables because of the hardness of your hearts. This time I will speak plainly because of your pigheadedness. IT'S NOT OUT THERE!"

**Gathering information is an outward affair,
but the path to realization is an inward journey.**

❰ ❰ ❰ ❰

*You can't teach something to a man.
You can only help him to discover it within himself.*
GALILEO

The Pond

✸ THE MASTER BROUGHT HIS disciples to the edge of a pond and began to teach them. "There is nowhere you need to go, there is nothing you need to do, to encounter God." "How then does it come about?" they asked. "The same way your reflection comes about," said the Master, "when you look into the pond."

As close as your reflection is to water,
God is to your Self.

❨ ❨ ❨ ❨

The wise who, by means of meditation on his Self, recognizes the Ancient,
who is difficult to be seen, who has entered into the dark, who is
hidden in the cave, who dwells in the abyss, as God...
KATHA UPANISHAD

True Courage

✶ A WAR BROKE OUT and the village was divided. Many enlisted for military service, whereas others became disillusioned and flocked to the monasteries. When the enemy was finally encroaching, a soldier took to the monasteries in a last attempt to gain recruits. He begged and pleaded with the monks to take up arms, but they refused. Finally, he appealed to the abbot. "Is your cowardice so great that you will not fight?" "On the contrary," said the abbot. "We are courageous not for fighting to survive, but for consenting to die."

☾ ☾ ☾ ☾

Die while you're alive and be absolutely dead.
Then do whatever you want; it's all good.
BUNAN

Who Is This Me?

✸ AS AN ATTEMPT TO FURTHER interfaith dialogue, the Master was invited to speak to a Western audience on the pre-existence of souls. At first, he was strongly opposed. "We do not share your pagan belief," they replied. "Rather, we believe that, before conception, the soul has no prior existence." Without another word, the Master, with great reverence, opened the Bible and began to read. "Sacrifice and offering you did not desire, but a body you prepared for me." Then, closing the book, he asked, "Now tell me, who is this 'me' of which your scriptures speak?"

❨ ❨ ❨ ❨

You are in error because you do not know the Scriptures or the
power of God. At the resurrection people will neither marry nor be
given in marriage; they will be like the angels in heaven.
[Since human beings are, in fact, embodied spirits.]
MATTHEW 22:29–30

Beyond Repair

✸ THE DISCIPLE PRAYED DAY and night that God would change his heart, but his prayer went unanswered. Confused and discouraged, he went to see the Master, who, after listening, seized an empty wineglass and hurled it to the floor, shattering it in pieces. "Can you repair it?" She asked. "Not a chance," replied the disciple. "The glass is unquestionably beyond repair, and must be replaced." The Master then turned to the disciple and said, "You are the glass."

**God is not in the business of restoring the old,
but ushering in the new.**

❮ ❮ ❮ ❮

*No one pours new wine into old wineskins. If he does, the wine will
burst the skins, and both the wine and the wineskins will be ruined.
No, he pours new wine into new wineskins.*
MARK 2:22

Light of the World

✳ A GROUP OF THEOLOGIANS got together to discuss whether Jesus had faith. The first argued that he had, and that he needed faith to overcome life's trials. The second argued from a different angle, that Jesus would not request the faith of others if he himself did not believe. The third theologian, who was not much for arguing, sat in silence. "What are your thoughts on the matter?" they asked. His reply:"When you come to believe you are the light of the world, what need have you of faith?"

Answer: as much as you have for a candle in daylight.

☾ ☾ ☾ ☾

… In Your light we see the light.
PSALM 36:10

Just Look

✸ WHEN ASKED BY A DISCIPLE if God was immanent or transcendent, the Master gave this response. "If I say God is transcendent, you will surely overlook Him. If I say he is immanent, you will not look close enough. If I say He is, you will ask me where He is, and if I answer here, you will still ask me where He is. So long as you look for Him, He cannot be found, but open your eyes and there is nowhere He is not."

Don't look for God, just look.

❨ ❨ ❨ ❨

In Him we live and move and have our being.
ACTS 17:28

No Door

✸ THE MASTER OFTEN SPOKE of prayer as going into your private room and closing the door. This form of prayer led to a peace that surpassed all understanding. Like the wind, it would come and go. Then one day, a disciple boldly asked whether it was possible to remain at peace. The Master replied, "See that there is no door."

When you see that there is no door
there is no entering or exiting.
There is no appearance or disappearance.
There is vastness only.

☾ ☾ ☾ ☾

Peace I leave with you; my peace I give you.
I do not give to you as the world gives.
Do not let your hearts be troubled and do not be afraid.
JOHN 14:27

Passing Away

❀ WHILE SCRIPTURE SCHOLARS ARGUED over whether or not enlightenment was also a Christian concept, the Dalai Lama stood up and read the following passage:

> **The time is short. From now on, those who have wives should live as if they had none; those who mourn, as if they did not; those who are happy, as if they were not; those who buy something, as if it were not theirs to keep; those who use the things of the world, as if not engrossed in them. For this world in its present form is passing away.**

When asked to comment, he replied, "These are the words of one who is enlightened."

❈ ❈ ❈ ❈

Among all living creatures there is no permanence.
SIDDHARTHA GAUTAMA

The Carpenter

✸ A TEAM OF JOURNALISTS was sent to a remote village to do a piece on a carpenter believed to be enlightened. They arrived, stayed for a few days, and left disappointed. When they returned home, immediately they were greeted by co-workers. "What was it like meeting one who is enlightened?" they asked. "Frankly," replied the journalists, "it was nothing out of the ordinary."

☾ ☾ ☾ ☾

If you become enlightened you will become so ordinary,
so simple, that nobody will take any note of you.
OSHO

Hiding

✸ THE DISCIPLE REACHED THE DOORSTEP of his Master and knocked at the door, but the Master did not answer. The disciple peered through the window, but the Master hid himself. He went around to the back entrance and beat upon the gate. Finally, the Master came out. "All the time you were inside, why didn't you answer?" He replied, "Because, more than my presence, you needed my absence. So I, like the Lord, hid myself to strengthen your resolve."

God is unknowable and yet known.
God is realized between these two dimensions.

☾ ☾ ☾ ☾

He is the most Manifest of the Manifest
and the most Hidden of the Hidden.
BAHA'U'LLAH

The Coin Toss

✷ TWO PROPHETS LIVED IN THE DESERT. One taught the way of realization, the other taught the way of repentance. Both had many followers and were renowned for their holiness and wisdom, but despite their similarities, they were thought to be at odds. Time passed and misunderstanding between the communities mounted. They sent for an arbitrator to settle the matter, and after some bickering, rather than continuing to quarrel, the two camps agreed to a coin toss to decide upon the true way. The arbitrator tossed the coin and the rest is legend. Some say it was mysteriously snatched out of the sky, and the two saw this as a sign to reconcile. Others, a bit more scrupulous, say that they simply came to see that there are two sides to every coin.

❨❨❨❨

*If religions are authentic, they contain the same elements of stability,
joy, peace, understanding, and love. The similarities as well as the
differences are there. They differ only in terms of emphasis.
Glucose and acid are in all fruits but their degrees differ.
We cannot say that one is a real fruit and the other is not.*
THICH NHAT HANH

The Content

✸ "BEFORE I MET MY MASTER, the content of my prayer was: fix it so I get what I want."

"And now?"

"Now it is: Fix it so I want what I get."

You will be content when you change the content of your prayer.

☾ ☾ ☾ ☾

Thy kingdom come, Thy will be done, on earth as it is in heaven.
THE LORD'S PRAYER

Back In School

✸ YEARS AFTER HE DROPPED OUT, the young man went back to school. As an undergraduate, he learned everything he could. He was now able to quote from memory theologians and poets, philosophers and saints. Afterward, he took to teaching and was praised for his great eloquence and knowledge. He showed such promise that many encouraged him to continue his education, and the following year he earned a doctorate. Soon, he became a preeminent scholar and began lecturing nationwide. Eventually, he was invited to lecture overseas. He began in France, then Germany, and made his way to the Far East where, for the first time, he met a yogi. "I have extensive knowledge, but little peace," said the scholar. "What should I do?" "Go back to school," replied the yogi. "You must be joking," said the scholar. "I am a Doctor of Sacred Theology and Philosophy and give lectures worldwide." "You have gone to school to learn," replied the yogi. "Now go back and unlearn."

The highest learning is unlearning.

❨ ❨ ❨ ❨

I have learned so much from God that I can no longer call
myself a Christian, a Hindu, a Moslem, A Buddhist, a Jew.
The Truth has shared so much of itself with me that I can no
longer call myself a man, a woman, an angel, or even pure Soul.
Love has befriended Hafiz so completely it has turned to ash
and freed me of every concept and image my mind has ever known.
HAFIZ

Making Bread

✸ DESIRING TO MAKE BREAD, a young girl purchased a cookbook. But after paging through hundreds of recipes, she only grew weary and more confused. In an attempt to end her distress, she brought her book to a nearby bakery. "I bought this cookbook, desiring to make bread," she explained, "but there are so many different recipes, and it is all so overwhelming." "May I see your book?" asked the baker. The girl handed over the cookbook. Opening the book, the baker said, "Start with this one. It has only the essential ingredients, without which, the dough would not rise."

**As there are many recipes for baking bread,
there are many paths to transformation. But,
like bread, there are also essential ingredients,
without which you would not rise.**

❨ ❨ ❨ ❨

*The fruit of silence is prayer. The fruit of prayer is faith.
The fruit of faith is love. The fruit of love is service.
The fruit of service is peace.*
MOTHER TERESA

The Movers

✸ AFTER MAKING EVERY CONCEIVABLE effort to move the odd-shaped desk through the doorway, the movers decided to take it apart. Within seconds, they dismantled the desk and carried it through with ease.

**As a skilled mover takes apart furniture to
move freely through the doorway, a wise man
dismantles beliefs to pass easily through life.**

❨ ❨ ❨ ❨

*Every time you make sense out of reality,
you bump into something that destroys the sense you made.*
ANTONY DE MELLO

Glimpsed

✸ A WOMAN CAME TO THE MASTER and posed this question: "Master, can the Truth be known?" "That depends what is meant by the question." "I don't understand," replied the woman. "Well," said the Master, "if you're asking whether the Truth can be known scientifically or philosophically, then undoubtedly, the answer is no. But if your question is if the Truth can be glimpsed, then the answer is, irrefutably, YES!"

☾ ☾ ☾ ☾

To see a world in a grain of sand, and heaven in a wildflower.
Hold infinity in the palm of your hand, and eternity in an hour.
WILLIAM BLAKE

Chained to a Post

WHEN THE CLEVER MAN ASKED if knowledge wasn't a good thing, the Master told the story of a dog who, chained to a post, was unable to reach its food. When pressed for an explanation, he replied, "You are the dog. The food is enlightenment, and the chain is your mind."

❰ ❰ ❰ ❰

He who is not aware of his ignorance
will be only misled by his knowledge.
RICHARD WHATLEY

Seeing

WHEN THE PLANET OF GREEN people settled on the planet Purple, they were met immediately with hostility and fear. The leaders, being themselves frightened, began a campaign and used propaganda to keep the others estranged. As a result, the communities grew segregated, and before long, they were rivals. On one occasion, a handicapped man wandered into enemy territory. Concerned, his family reported him missing, and a rescue operation was devised to reunite the disabled man with his kin. When the rescue team arrived, to their astonishment they found the man drinking and having the time of his life. Judging him to be a spy, they seized the man and straightway put him in prison. Not long after, the public defender came with the family to request the man be released. "On what grounds?" they asked. The public defender replied, "My client is blind."

The whole of the human vocation can be summed up in just one word, SEEING.

❨ ❨ ❨ ❨

It is only with the heart that one sees clearly;
what is essential is invisible to the human eye.
ANTOINE DE EXUPERY

One Thing More Beautiful

✹ WHEN THE MASTER TURNED FIFTY, her disciples commemorated the occasion with a surprise party. They rented a hall, catered in food, and flew in guests to celebrate the big event. When she discovered this had been done, the Master was deeply touched and moved to tears. "There's just one thing more beautiful than thoughtfulness," she said. "What's that?" they asked. "Being thoughtless."

Man lives in paradise until interrupted by thought.

☾ ☾ ☾ ☾

You follow thought, and it takes you away from home.
ARJUNA ARDAGH

The Length of the Road

✳ TO EACH NEWCOMER, THE MASTER posed this question: "What is the length of the road?" "Which road?" they asked. "Any road," he replied. Confused and bewildered, the disciples looked to one another, each more baffled than the next. Sensing their discomfort, at last the Master spoke up. "It is exactly the length of the stones and no more."

When the stones come to an end,
the road comes to an end.
When thoughts come to an end,
you come to an end.

☾ ☾ ☾ ☾

Only let the moving waters calm down,
and the sun and moon will be reflected
on the surface of your being.
RUMI

The Transport

✸ WHEN NEWS CAME THAT THE POPE was coming to India, a villager was asked to design a transport. After several days, he returned with a specialized and highly modified rickshaw. Before he agreed to purchase the transport, the bishop expressed some concerns. "Where will his Holiness put his luggage?" he asked. The villager walked around to the back and revealed a large compartment. Then came a second question. "What will protect his Grace from the sun?" The villager then pulled a latch, revealing a sleek convertible top. Then, came a third question. "How fast does it go?" At that, the villager invited the bishop aboard and took off with great speed. "Whoa!" he shouted. Immediately, the transport came to a halt. "What is it?" the villager asked. "The ride is terribly bumpy," said the bishop. "What is to absorb the shocks?" "His beliefs," the villager replied.

**When our beliefs absorb the shocks of life,
do we really do justice to our sorrows?**

❨ ❨ ❨ ❨

*The ending of sorrow begins with the facing of psychological facts
within oneself and being totally aware of all the implications of
those facts from moment to moment. This means never escaping
that one is in sorrow, never rationalizing it, never offering an
opinion about it, but living with that fact completely.*
J. KRISHNAMURTI

Two Colleagues

THERE WERE TWO COLLEAGUES. One gained recognition and world acclaim. The other longed for the least acknowledgement, but did not get it. Over time, the latter grew bitter and green with envy, and in an attempt to even the playing field, devised a plan to sabotage his colleague's success. He plotted for months and was about to enact his crooked scheme, when he was approached by a homeless man in tattered clothes. "Just one thing keeps you from experiencing the happiness you seek," said the street mystic. "What's that? he asked. "Comparison."

Comparison is the surest path to feeling cheated.

❨ ❨ ❨ ❨

Not everybody can be famous, but everybody can be great.
DR. MARTIN LUTHER KING, JR.

Another Illusion

TO TEST THE LEARNING of a certain disciple, the Master appeared first as a beggar, second as a banker, and third as a beautiful woman. Within the course of an hour, the disciple ignored the beggar, deceived the banker, and slept with the beautiful woman. Moments later, the Master showed up on the disciple's doorstep. "You've spent years studying. What have you to show for it?" The disciple excused himself and returned with a handful of diplomas and certificates. The Master seized the lot and set the combustible collection on fire. "What in heaven's name are you doing?" the disciple shouted. The Master replied, "Liberating you from yet another illusion."

An infallible sign of learning is not what you've read or studied, but how you spend your day.

☾ ☾ ☾ ☾

The proper use of education is to engage in more wholesome action.
TENZIN GYATSO

Three Monks

✦ THREE MONKS LIVED in a monastery. One monk prayed before a statue of the Buddha, another before an image of the Madonna, and the eldest knelt before the Infant of Prague. When asked by the others why he showed such devotion to the infant, the eldest replied. "I kneel here as a constant reminder." "A reminder of what?" they asked. "That although experience belongs to the aged, wisdom comes to the innocent and young."

☾ ☾ ☾ ☾

Amen, I say to you, unless you turn and become like children,
you will not enter the kingdom of heaven.
MATTHEW 18:3

The Fear of Hell

✺ WHILE AN ANGELIC EXPRESSION shone on the Master's face, a disciple approached and asked whether or not she feared hell. Still deep in meditation, the Master opened her eyes, gracefully gestured, and replied, "For one who has overcome the world, hell is no longer." "What becomes of it?" the disciple asked. "With everything else," said the Master, "it disappears when one enters the heart."

**The closest heaven is the heart,
the nearest hell; the mind.**

☾ ☾ ☾ ☾

*The coming of the Kingdom of God cannot be observed and
no one will announce, "Look here it is or there it is.
For behold the Kingdom of heaven is (within) (among) (upon) you.*
LUKE 18:20

For the First Time

❂ WHEN CHAOS ENSUED at a local university, the board sought help from the outside. After just days, they agreed to a new principal, whose methods were thought to be somewhat avant garde. Unlike his predecessors, the new principal held freedom in the highest esteem, and rather than impose additional structures and prohibitions, he simply removed pre-existing ones. Within a matter of months, there was perfect order. "How did you know the students would react the way they have?" the board asked. "They have not reacted at all," he replied, "but acted for the first time."

The moment you stop reacting out of unconsciousness you start acting from Intelligence.

❰ ❰ ❰ ❰

You don't need conscience when you have consciousness
ANTONY DE MELLO

Through Me

✳ AFTER A BRIEF SOJOURN on Earth, the Master died and was taken to heaven, where she was warmly greeted by Jesus. "Come," said Jesus, "blessed of my Father and inherit the Kingdom prepared for you from the foundation of the world. For I was hungry and you gave me food. I was thirsty and you gave me drink, a stranger and you welcomed me, naked and you clothed me, ill and you cared for me, in prison and you visited me." Completely dumfounded, the woman replied, "I did no such thing, Lord. You yourself did it through me."

❨ ❨ ❨ ❨

One must realize that he is not the doer, but that he is only
a tool of some Higher Power. Let that Higher Power do what
is inevitable and let me act only according to its dictates.
The actions are not mine, therefore the results cannot be mine either.
SRI RAMANA MAHARSHI

A New Humanity

⚛ AFTER A GLOBAL NUCLEAR WAR, a few survivors thought to print a new Bible. All exhortations and commandments were left out. It consisted of events, beautiful discourses, paradoxical phrases and parables, but no directives or commentary. Not a single pronouncement or counsel could be found, except that which was implicit. As a result, arguing ceased, judgment fell away, legalism died, and guilt disappeared. For the first time, no one knew what God expected. They had to think for themselves. When the multitude of heavenly hosts saw this, they turned and asked, "Are you going to send a savior?" "Why bother?" said God. "They are already loving." "Besides, remember what happened last time."

**The problem is not authority, but authoritarianism:
the arrogant belief that insists, "you know."**

☾ ☾ ☾ ☾

*All the harm that befalls the world comes from a failure to
understand the truths of Scripture in all their true clarity.*
ST. TERESA OF AVILA

The Mountain

❀ THE MASTER LED HIS DISCIPLES up a mountain and began to teach them. "If you have faith the size of a mustard seed, you can say to this mountain, 'Be uprooted and tossed into the sea,' and it will be done for you." Some time after, his closest friends wanted to question him about the meaning, but no one did. Finally, a stranger in the crowd inquired. The Master replied, "Faith is the belief that something lies behind the mountain." "The mountain," he added, "represents every obstacle to Self or god-realization. By grace they are removed either one rock at a time or all at once. How it happens makes no difference, but that it happens is essential. Then when the mountain (of ego) is uprooted and hurled into the sea (of being), it is no longer a mountain. Rather it becomes the sea." Fully satisfied with the response, he replied, "Master, you have the words of eternal life."

**Whereas you are eternal, the mountain
of your personality accumulated in time.**

❰ ❰ ❰ ❰

Christ is the same yesterday and today and forever.
HEBREWS 13:8

Up a Tree

✳ THE MASTER SAT DOWN and addressed the masses with these words: "You are not the mind, neither are you the body." While he was in mid-sentence, one from the crowd unleashed a fierce tiger, and within seconds, the Master was up a tree. When a follower heard of the incident, he remarked, "If it is true that we are not the body, why did you flee?" "Allow me to clarify," said the Master. "We are not the body, exclusively."

❰ ❰ ❰ ❰

In the beginning one has to be told that he is not the body because he thinks he is the body only, whereas he is the body and all else.
SRI RAMANA MAHARSHI

No Mind

✷ AFTER YEARS OF MEDITATION, the Master concluded that the mind didn't exist. When he made this discovery, he fell silent and took to writing. Not long after, his name gained recognition and he developed a large following. Eventually, his popularity grew and he established an ashram where others could come to the same realization. Within months, there was a thriving community. Word spread and a certain man abandoned his family, sold his possessions, and went in search of the ashram. When the Master learned of this, he was deeply disturbed and greeted the man, saying, "Have you completely lost your mind?" "There is no mind," he replied. "In this case," said the Master, "it appears you are right."

"No mind," does not mean "no brain."
It simply means that mind is no longer
limited or dominated by the ego.

☾ ☾ ☾ ☾

The essence of mind is only awareness or consciousness. When the ego,
however, dominates it, it functions as the reasoning, thinking or sensing
faculty. The cosmic mind, not being limited by the ego, has nothing separate
from itself and is therefore only aware.
SRI RAMANA MAHARSHI

The Basics

✹ INSPIRED BY A CERTAIN TEXT, the young woman made up her mind to renounce the world. She sold her possessions, gave her money to the poor, and shaved her head to commemorate the moment. But as time went by, there remained a persistent hankering for the past, and eventually she grew discouraged. At the advice of a friend, she went to see the Master, known for her insight into the mystery of life and human nature. With great compassion, the Master looked upon the woman's poor constitution and tense features, then taking her by the hand, sat her down for a sumptuous feast. When they had eaten and had their fill, the Master spoke. "Daughter, your whole problem is that you've not yet learned the basics." The Master then asked the woman to recite the alphabet and stopped her at the letter L. "You see," she said, "even alphabetically, delight comes before denial."

❨ ❨ ❨ ❨

I have come that they may have life, and have it to the full.
JOHN 10:10

Her Fondest Treasure

❋ EACH DAY, THE RICH OLD WOMAN would put on a different hat and parade around the neighborhood. Now her taste was so poor that as time went on the hats managed to get uglier and uglier, until one day the youngest daughter couldn't take it any more and spoke her mind. When confronted, the eldest wanted to say the same thing but did not have the heart. Not wishing to hurt her mother's feelings, she resorted to flattery instead. Soon after, the woman died and the estate was divided. To the youngest she left the china, the rugs, and the furniture. To the eldest, she left her fondest treasure: the collection of hats.

If you didn't flatter, if you didn't embellish, if you didn't sensor what you wanted to say, you would be that much closer to embodying Truth.

☾ ☾ ☾ ☾

Let your 'Yes' mean 'Yes,' and your 'No' mean 'No.'
Anything more is from the evil one.
MATTHEW 5:37

The Anagram

✴ WHILE WALKING THROUGH a cemetery, the disciple's eyes fell upon the headstone of a great saint. Inscribed was a portrait of his smiling face along with the words: "For Nothing has ever existed." Overcome by meaninglessness, the disciple became withdrawn. Sensing that it was the epitaph on the headstone, the Master approached and said, "Like an anagram, it may help if you rearrange the letters." The Master then wrote out the epitaph, cut out the words, and reset them. "See, Nothing has forever existed."

**Between the notes of a symphony
there is NOTHING.
Between every word and thought
there is NOTHING.
Before birth and death
there is NOTHING.
Before conception and creation
there was NOTHING.**

☾ ☾ ☾ ☾

*God is a pure no-thing concealed in now and here.
The less you reach for him, the more he will appear.*
ANGELUS SILESIUS

The Inverted Way

✹ WHEN A VILLAGER MENTIONED that he could solve the riddle while standing on his head, the Master held him to it. When he explained that the expression was idiomatic, the Master did not yield, but insisted the villager accept the challenge. Once the man was inverted, the Master gave the riddle. "Who is standing on his head?" At once the villager's mind went blank and he could not answer. "To find out," said the Master, "you must invert your mind, not your body." He then added the following words: "Stop trying, and you will succeed. Stop searching, and you will find. Stop acquiring, and you will have. Stop traveling, and you will arrive. Such is the inverted way."

Reality is right side up.
Your mind is what's upside down.

☾ ☾ ☾ ☾

Wonder of wonders, marvel of marvels, human beings are already enlightened. But because men's minds have become inverted through delusive thinking they fail to perceive this.
SIDDHARTHA GAUTAMA

Only Awareness Remains

✳ A GROUP OF VILLAGERS went to a support group and invited the Master to join them. When they arrived, they greeted one another and straightway began to share stories. All were struggling with essentially the same problem, that of how to deal with the monkey on their back. Finally, they asked the Master for any insight. The Master paused, looked about, then told a story. "A scientist went to the jungle to study monkeys. As soon as he arrived, he spotted one and watched it intensely. As he looked, he became acutely aware of the monkey's fondness for bananas. He became aware of how the monkey would climb, swing from trees, and go to great lengths to get the fruit, and when he got the fruit he noticed how the two became one. The banana was not separate from the monkey, and the monkey was not separate from the banana." The message is this: If a monkey is on your back, you must place the monkey before you and watch it like a scientist. Then you will see that the seeker and what is sought are one. When this is known, attachment is ended and only awareness remains.

When you look without thought there is
no judgement, no commentary, no craving.
When you see that the observer
and the observed are one, both are dropped,
and only Awareness remains.
Then and only then is sound judgement possible.

☾ ☾ ☾ ☾

The lamp of the body is the eye. If your eye is sound
your whole body will be filled with light,
but if your eye is bad your whole body will be in darkness.
And if the light in you is darkness, how great will the darkness be.
MATTHEW 6:22–23

One

❂ AN OBSCURE POET FELL into realization and wrote the following poem. When the villagers read it, there were mixed feelings. Some were indifferent, some were inspired, and still others took offense.

> When you realize the Self, mind falls away
> When mind falls away, ego falls away
> When ego falls away, separateness falls away.
> When you rest as Self, mind is not
> When you remain as Self, ego is not
> When you are just your Self, separation is not
> You and God are ONE.

Years passed and the anonymous poem was discovered. Not knowing what to make of it, scholars were summoned to determine who wrote it. Some ascribed it to Buddha, some said Lao-Tsu, and still others attributed it to Jesus Christ. When a good amount of time had passed, they were undecided, and so agreed to put the names into a hat. They reached in and pulled one out. It read, "The Spirit of Truth."

The containers are many, but the content is one.

☾ ☾ ☾ ☾

In all ten directions of the universe there is only one truth.
When we see clearly the great teachings are the same.
What can ever be lost? What can be attained?
If we attain something it was there from the beginning of time.
If we lose something it is hiding somewhere near us.
RYOKAN

A Brief Sermon

✷ KNOWING HIS TIME WAS SHORT, the Master led his disciples up a hilltop stretched out his arms and delivered a brief and final sermon. "You are the light of the world." When he finished, he immediately picked up his walking stick, turned and headed down the hill. "Stunned at the brevity of his words, the disciples fell silent. Knowing they wanted to question him the Master paused then stopped dead in his tracks. "You've imparted to us this knowledge before, Master, but what do we do with it?" "Why do you complicate what is simple?" He replied. "Just shine little children, just shine."

You're always asking, "What am I to do?"
Well, what does light do?
Answer: It shines.

☾ ☾ ☾ ☾

Let your light shine before men, that they may see your
good deeds and praise your Father in heaven.
MATTHEW 5:16

Wisdom Literature from White Cloud Press

Apprentice of the Heart by Guy Finley
ISBN: 1-883991-58-7 / Paperback: $14.95

Everything Starts From Prayer
Mother Teresa's Meditations on Spiritual Life for People of All Faiths
Selected and arranged by Anthony Stern, MD
ISBN: 1-883991-37-4 / Paperback: $12.95

The Vision: Reflections on the Way of the Soul
Translated by Juan R.I. Cole
ISBN: 1-833991-02-1 / Cloth: $17

Green Sea of Heaven: Fifty ghazals from the Diwan of Hafiz
Translated by Elizabeth T. Gray, Jr.
ISBN: 1-883991-06-4 / Paperback: $14.95

Physicians of the Soul: The Psychologies of the World's Great
Spritual Teachers by Robert May, Ph.D.
ISBN: 1-883991-42-0 / Paperback: $16.95

Wisdom of the Master: The Spiritual Teachings of 'Abu'l-Baha
by 'Abu'l-Baha
ISBN: 1-883991-23-4 / Cloth: $10.95

For more information on these and other titles, visit:
www.whitecloudpress.com

About the Author

✸ KEVIN EDWARDS holds a Master's degree in Sacred Theology from the Angelicum in Rome with an emphasis on Transformative Spirituality and Mysticism. A gifted writer, speaker, poet, and storyteller, he invites his audience to re-evaluate their vision of themselves, their vision of the world, and their vision of God. No stranger to other cultures, Kevin has enlightened audiences in Rome, the U.S., and India, where he received the name Prakash, which means light.